P.O.V.

A Personal Perspective of the Bible

Volume 2

C. P. CLARKE

The characters and events portrayed in this book are based on the accounts written down in the Bible and creative license has been used to expand on the stories retold.

Cover design by: The Smithy Creative

www.thesmithycreative.co.uk

Other titles by the author:

    Life In Shadows

    Stalking The Daylight

    The Killing

    Vicky Rivers

    Furi'on

    POV - Volume 1

    A Question of Faith

    Stories on a Wall

www.cpclarke-author.com

This book is dedicated to my son J.J who continues to be my biggest fan and has been the testing ground for every story.

It is also dedicated to my beautiful daughter Amy Elise, and to my extended family in Uganda: Osborn and Patricia, in whom I am well proud.

C. P. CLARKE

CONTENTS

C. P. CLARKE

Preface

In writing this book, and its previous volume, I have found the process of trying to get into the heads of the various biblical characters, attempting to see things from their Point Of View to get a personal perspective, a fascinating way of understanding the Bible. It has helped me greatly in understanding what those characters (both the famed, the lesser known, and in some case imagined, ordinary people) went through, creating an opportunity to discover the emotions and motivations behind all those stories we read in the Bible and take for granted as we glance over them in our daily readings, or retell them to our children or to various church groups. By lengthening the story and bringing the characters alive it allows us to grasp more clearly what the original writers were trying to convey, it allows us to relate and identify with personality traits, and it hopefully helps us to remember the story and its purpose within the bigger picture that is the Bible as a whole.

I have tried where possible to keep as close to scripture as I can in my re-telling of the stories, however, it has been necessary at times to conjure imaginative scenarios and motives in order to fit in with the characters. In some cases the scenarios presented before me were multiple and so I was forced to choose a path to go down (as in David and Bathsheba's affair being consensual rather than forced). Not everyone will agree with the route I've taken but as far as I can tell the creative line I've gone down in these re-tellings does not contradict scripture.

I found writing this book (which I did in between writing the novel Furi'on) more challenging than Volume 1, partly due to the first volume having been mostly written before I decided to collate my stories for what would become the first of the POV series of books, but mostly I found it challenging because my number one fan (my son J.J) was champing at the bit for new stories. I remember making the mistake, whilst writing Dreamer, of reading to him each new chapter as I wrote it, which left him frustrated as I would keep stopping to make corrections, and he would then be expectant of the next section which I would then have to find time to write quickly to keep up with the demand.

I am pleased to say that J.J's enthusiasm for the stories hasn't dissipated and he is eager for me to begin work on Volume 3. I am also pleased to say that both my children were great advocates in flogging copies of Volume 1 to their friends and teachers! So get back out there selling guys!

The money made from Volume 1, and one of the main reasons the kids were so keen to sell it, was all donated to sending a team from our church to Uganda to work with Watoto Church, something I have done a number of times, but on this occasion my whole family were part of the team. The reason I mention this here is because we had the great opportunity of meeting our two sponsored children in Laminadera Children's Village in Gulu, and I/we were greatly impacted by meeting them and seeing the impact Watoto has had on their lives and how they are being raised in that environment to love and trust in Jesus. This is why I have dedicated this book, not only to my own children, but also to our sponsored children, my extended family in Uganda.

The ideas for Volume 3 are already swimming through my mind, so I'm sure my number one fan won't have to wait long for my next take on what the Bible has to tell us.

C. P. CLARKE

C. P. CLARKE

DREAMER
(GENESIS 30-50)

Rachel:

I can die happy. I have given birth to a son; a second child to make my husband proud. Long have we walked the ridge of our relationship, teetering on the edge as we struggled for balance on that lonely clifftop of love. So long did it take us to be joined in marriage as my father blocked the way for his own selfish gain. Then I lost him to my own sister, she marrying him and bearing him children. Even when my beloved finally won me I disappointed him. I failed him in delivering him a child and I feared to lose him completely. My jealousy over my sister almost overwhelmed me then, but God was gracious and merciful and Joseph was eventually born to me. He was one of many of my husband's heirs but he was the first born to me, whom he loved, and from the start my love doted on this son as though he were the favourite of his kin, for he was born out of the love we shared together. And now he has another, Ben-Oni I have named him, but his father wishes him to be known as Benjamin, the youngest of his children. I will not live long to see him grow beyond the day of his birth for the blood doesn't cease to flow and the pain does not subside now that my boy has taken his first breaths. I will not see either of my boys grow to men but I am confident for their future, for they are in good hands with their father to watch over them and their siblings to play with. Yes, I can die happy now and go peacefully to my God who has been faithful to me.

Joseph:

I really must lay off the cheese before bed. I had yet another wild dream last night. It wasn't the same as before but similar. In this dream I wasn't in the field with my brothers as I was last time, where we were gathering sheaves of grain and mine rose upright while my brothers' eleven sheaves all bowed to mine. No, in this dream the sun and moon and eleven stars were bowing down to me. It was really vivid and had that sense of meaning to it that set it apart from the usual type of dreams I get. It's really hard to explain but I think it means something, I just don't know what.

I made the mistake, again, of trying to tell my father all about it. I should have learnt my lesson from the first time and spoken to him in private, what was I thinking telling him over breakfast with my brothers listening in. They all hate me as it is, especially since they know I told my father about their slacking out in the field. So what if I dobbed them in, why should my father's business suffer because of their laziness? Of course that was just one incident that I'd reported on, but it wasn't the only thing they were upset with me about.

I'm special, my father always tells me so, and they are just so jealous because I am better than they and my father honours me by granting my every request. It's rare for him to rebuke me or deny me what I want, even when he is reluctant I usually know how to get round him; beyond the tough old exterior he's a big softie at heart. He really put me in my place this morning, though. Of course he knew about the previous dream about the sheaves and how when we were out tending the flocks my brothers had reacted angrily and threatened to beat me to a pulp rather than be ruled over by me, for that was how they interpreted the dream. When I had told my father about the incident he had pulled them all aside and had words about threatening me. "Why must you always speak so badly of him and accost him in such a manner?" I heard him bellow at them. "Leave the boy alone, he has done no harm. Why do you threaten him so?" They laid off me for a couple of days after that, so I figured all was good and that my father would stand up for me again. Boy was I wrong.

When I told them all this morning about the sun, moon and stars I felt like my father had slapped me across the face when he reacted so badly, telling me not to be so arrogant and spoilt. "What is this dream you had? Do you really think we will all bow down to the ground before you?" My father was angry yet nevertheless thoughtful on the matter, my brothers on the other hand laughed almost uncontrollably at my stupidity, and there was a vicious scowling behind their eyes and their upturned mouths revealed sharp snarling teeth. "Seventeen years we've had to put up with this joker, this pathetic dreamer," I heard one of them say out of earshot of my father. "How much longer?" I heard another mumble in reply.

I really don't get why they are so angry with me. It was just a dream. It's not like I was saying I wanted them to bow down to me. Nor was I saying that was what the dream meant; that was just their interpretation and my father's, not mine.

I think I'll keep my head down for a couple of days until this all blows over and hopefully they'll forget all about it. I know my father won't be angry with me for long and I'm sure he'll tell the others to take it easy on me. Maybe next time I'll try and figure out what the dream means myself before talking to them about it. I'm sure if I ask him God would reveal its true meaning.

Reuben:

Here comes that arrogant little snot dawdling away in the distance. He's just aimlessly prancing about without a care in the world, daydreaming, staring at the clouds with no sense of urgency in his step. You wouldn't think that he'd been sent here to help us. He wouldn't be here at all if he hadn't been sent by our father; too often does the boy think it's beneath him to work in the field. Actually, I bet he's been sent to spy on us again, to check we're doing our job and not slacking. I don't know why dad trusts him and not us. We all do our bit but all Joseph cares about is what the old man thinks.

The others have noticed him now. It's hard to miss that blasted coat of his! It cost the old man a fortune getting all the fine material and rich ornaments to make the design stand out. None of us knew what the old man was up to at first as he slaved away at the coat, delicately designing and sowing together the material himself. He'd made us each coats before but none so exquisite and lavish as this. It's so dazzlingly beautiful it's almost ugly. No one can help but notice Joseph when he's wearing it, but then I guess that was the point our father was trying to make: the old man wants him to stand out among us, his favourite son of his favourite wife; he doesn't want him to be lost in the squad of brutish lads that are his brood. If his mother were still alive then maybe we would complain more about the injustice of it all, but none of us want to speak badly of Rachel's offspring for the loss of her still weighs heavily on the old man.

I'm amazed he managed to find us out here. We are a good distance from home and much further than we'd told the old man we would go. As far as he knew we were grazing the flocks out near Shechem, but Dotham, where we are now, is a good 13 miles north of there. Joseph has done well to find us. Despite all his faults he can be quite resourceful at times. Any one of us probably would have headed back home when seeing we had moved on from Shechem, but Joseph is nothing but obedient to the commands of his father.

Judah:

"Here comes that dreamer!" I said nudging Reuben, but he had already spotted him in the distance and was eyeing him like a hawk studying his prey. "We should get rid of him while we have the chance," I muttered, "So far from home who is to know?"

The wind caught my words and as I turned I could see my thoughts registering in the eyes of my brothers who were all stopping one by one as the coat far off in the distance sparkled under the mid-day sun as he traipsed across the fields that edged around the city of Dothan. "We could throw him into one of those cisterns and say that a ferocious animal devoured him," I suggested, looking back at one of the dug wells behind us. The others looked also, and for a moment I thought they would pounce on me for the suggestion and I was ready to laugh it off as a joke or the madness of the mid-day sun (I think now that's maybe what overcame us all). When they turned back there was murder in their eyes and the hunger of wolves snarling and drooling amongst the sheep.

"We'll see what comes of his dreams then," sniggered Levi.

"No!" It was Reuben who objected and accosted us for our ill thoughts. He shared our contempt for Joseph but argued that it would be wrong to spill his blood, he was still our brother after all. We all listened to Reuben; being the eldest he carried more weight and authority than the rest of us and was loathe to upset the old man unnecessarily if he could avoid it. I could see the cogs of his mind trying to work a way that he could do away with

Joseph and yet gain favour with the old man by rescuing his favoured son. I could see through his plans of coming back for him and knew where that would leave the rest of us in the eyes of our father. I wasn't going to leave Reuben any wriggle room if I could help it; whatever plan we hatched we would all take the credit and all share the guilt, Reuben included. But Reuben had spoken and already the blood lust was dissipating from the lips of my brothers.

We argued it out between us, eventually agreeing that we would rough up the dreamer to teach him a lesson and throw him into one of the dry cisterns for a couple of days. He wouldn't be able to climb out on his own and we could come back and get him out before beginning the journey back home

By the time Joseph reached us our plan was hatched. We gave him a good beating and stripped off his coat, literally ripping it from his back. For those few minutes we had turned savage as we launched upon him as wolves attacking one of our own sheep.

Our flocks were split across the range so Reuben had gone off to gather any strays and herd them together on the far hill for the night and return in the morning; eager he was to set off for home. I knew he was uncomfortable about leaving Joseph in the well and would hang back to get him out once we headed back home to Bethel. I talked it over with the others but none of us could see a way of being rid of Joseph permanently without going against Reuben.

We hunkered down for supper as the evening light dimmed and the air around us cooled. Off in the distance we could see a caravan train taking the path south across the land.

"Merchants!" whispered Dan, the one word full of meaning that wasn't lost on any of us. We all looked to each other in silent debate and within moments it was decided. We split in two, one group heading off to flag down the caravan and the others racing back to the well to pull out Joseph and make him presentable.

It turned out the caravan was heading for Egypt. We couldn't believe our luck. We thought it might have been following the coast down to Philistia, but Egypt was even further, and the further the better. These guys were Ishmaelites coming from Gilead and their camels were loaded up with spices, balm, and myrrh ready to sell to the Egyptians. The smell was incredible. You couldn't smell the usual stink of the camels as the air around them was perfumed. It didn't take us long to proposition them on the sale of a slave, and on seeing the fine young specimen of Joseph (admittedly he wasn't bad looking and in the prime of his youth) these shrewd traders could see that they could make an easy profit on the boy in foreign lands. They made us an offer and after a short period of haggling we agreed on a price of 20 shekels of silver, handed over our brother (whom we'd gagged to silence his protests), bid farewell to the Ishmaelites and then went back to our supper.

I wish I could say that I felt guilty, but at the time I didn't; I was just looking forward to seeing the look on Reuben's face when he realised Joseph was gone.

Reuben:

"Is there any breakfast for me?" I called to my brothers as I steered the sheep their way. I got a wave and a nod in return and a hand pointing to the tent where our food was kept. A small fire was burning outside it and the scraps of breakfast were scattered around makeshift seats on the floor. I grabbed a morsel of food for myself and a larger portion to take over to the well. "I'm just going to take over something for the boy," I yelled back. I knew they wouldn't have fed him and I wanted Joseph to know

I had taken care of him; it was important he reported favourably of me when he complained to our father about the way his brothers had treated him.

At first I thought I had the wrong cistern, and then I thought maybe they had moved him to another, and then again thought that maybe they had had sympathy with him in the night and let him sleep in the tent. For a brief moment my heart was glad and I thought the day would turn out well, and then I turned around.

"Why are you all stood there staring at me?" I asked. They shifted on their feet uncomfortably and gave each other curious guilty glances. "Well?" I asked, "Is someone going to tell me what's going on? Where is our brother, Joseph?"

"Did you see the caravan last night?" Levi offered up.

I nodded, a knot tightening in the pit of my stomach. "Midianites they looked to me," I commented.

"They will be far off by now for they were travelling through the night on their way to Egypt," said Judah.

I shook my head. "No! What have you done?" But it was obvious what they had done and there was no way of catching the merchants and paying them back what they had paid, not that they would sell him back for such a meager price, for he was worth far more than that to them.

I sank to my knees. How was I to return home to my father, Jacob? How could I tell him the truth that his sons had colluded to get rid of his favoured one? How could I convince him I had nothing to do with it? He would never believe me and as the eldest I would be held responsible for the actions of the others. "Where can I turn now?" I cried.

"Don't worry, brother, we have thought about this and we have a plan," said Judah pulling me to my feet.

Jacob:

There is blood on my hands, but it's not mine. The garments I hold are torn and soiled, blood seeps through the material where I have tried to wash it off, where I have tried to mend the fabric, as though sewing it together will bring him back. Caked and crumpled from its day's journey buried in the sack of Reuben's camel. They all hung back while he broke the news. There was no body to return home, no bones to be buried.

I recognised the coat immediately. How could I not? I'd spent so much time and effort putting it together; I knew its every detail. "This is Joseph's coat'" I said confused, looking passed Reuben as the count of his brothers stood behind him, but I could see no sign of the young lad I'd sent out to the field to join his older kin. Quickly I put the pieces together as I looked back to Reuben and stated, half questioningly hoping he would contradict my conclusion, "Surely a ferocious animal has devoured him and he has been torn to pieces." Reuben didn't deny it, nor did the others. They said nothing in response but hung their heads in sadness with tears of loss on their cheeks.

I let out a scream then, a gut wrenching bellow that ripped out from my insides as I tore my tunic from my chest, ripping it wide apart with my bare hands as the pain of death consumed me. Oh, I wish I could have died in my son's place. He had so much to live for. He had so many fine qualities that would see him well in life: he was handsome and smart, caring and full of fun. Admittedly he had his faults, as do we all: he was arrogant, but to that fault I take the blame for I mollycoddled him and bolstered his ego by showering him with too much love and affection so that he saw himself above the others. In that I ruined him, but he had so much more our Lord God could use him for.

I stripped what remained of my clothes and put on sackcloth. The family circled round me trying to comfort me but I was having none of it; I will not be comforted in my pain while my son is lost to me, I would rather spend the rest of my days in mourning.

Potiphar:

A fine price I paid, oh yes, a fine price indeed. He was worth every penny. The slave market was teeming with foreigners with fresh bodies brought in by the traders who came from all over. There were men there blacker than the night who had followed the River Nile from Africa's heartlands to Upper Egypt and flaunting their wares all the way to Lower Egypt's golden cost line. There were women and children among the slaves brought up from various tribes but none suited my purpose; mostly they were uneducated or brutish in their demeanor, but I was after something a touch more civilised. Few came from the western lands of the Mediterranean due to the emerging growing economies of empiric states being birthed in those not so distant lands. Then there were these rough nomadic tribes from the east with their skin more akin to ours, being not so dark and yet not so pale that they easily blended in (so long as you smoothed off the roughness of their scraggly hair and beards). Many of them crossed the Red Sea at its thinnest stretch or rode camel trains across the Desert of Shur, the slave handlers having acquired their products on route at the lesser known cities at a bargain price knowing that we Egyptian's would pay well for quality servants.

I ramble, forgive me, let me speak favourably of my new purchase. I am so pleased with him! He is young, in his late teens and barely growing any facial hair - it will be little effort to convince him to remain clean shaven if he wishes to be accepted in his new land. He is strong and handsome: a fine specimen - I felt his arms and legs; he has worked the land and knows of farming and no stranger to having to walk long distances in the heat. His jaw is strong with all teeth accounted for and no obvious blemish or scarring to disfigure him. In appearance he is impeccable.

I almost lost him, all be said, had I arrived a moment later to the market I would have seen the back of Ahmose, the royal astrologer, walking off with my prize. Ahmose had seen what had drawn me immediately to the boy: it wasn't his good looks but that sparkle in his eye, that intent deep obedience to his situation and observance of his surroundings - I saw intelligence. In truth I'm not a small man, not with strength in stature (not any more at any rate, I've let myself go a bit since being made captain of the guard; too much feasting at Pharaoh's expense) but these days I'm wider in girth than I'd like to admit, if you get my meaning, so nudging and barging my way through a crowd has become second nature for one of my size and command of authority. So seeing Ahmose make his beeline for the same slave trader I quickly beat my path to it in time to clasp the boy's wrist as a first claim of interest. I knew I had to bid high on my first price or Ahmose, who was still waiting in the wings, would try to usurp the sale from under me, not that he would challenge me directly, for my position is one of power and good royal guards are harder to come by than star gazers, of which we have plenty.

I took home my new purchase at once and had him cleaned up and adorned in attire suitable for our culture and his new position as household servant. Joseph his name is, hailing from Bethel in the land of Canaan. He is polite enough and well mannered. I have mind to set him some tasks to see what he is capable of.

***

Well Joseph has proven his worth a hundred times what I paid for him. He is as devout to his servitude in my house as he is to the god he worships, and his god is clearly with him in everything he sets his hand to. He had served as my own personal attendant for some time, a role in which I was well pleased, so a short while ago I set him as head of my household hoping that this blessing he carries with him would rub off in every area of my home. To my delight not only is my home flourishing under his watchful eye (I have left everything in his care and have entrusted him with all I have, so confident am I in his abilities and devotion) but also my fields are doing well and my purse is growing fat, and I feel that his blessing is most certainly on me also.

Mrs Potiphar:

It is fair to say that of late I have been bored of my husband. He has grown portly and lazy. When I married him he was a strong energetic soldier full of ambition and mindful of pleasing me in all ways as we embraced our young love. Now he barely pays me the time of day as he spends his time scratching the backs of Pharaoh's court officials as he secures his political status and financial purse in case anyone tries to oust him from his position. I have become little but a token on his arm at banquets and festivals; he forgets that I have needs too. The world is not all about money and power, there is love and romance too, or failing that just simply time and attention. In the absence of these is there any wonder I've begun to look elsewhere to fill the void of passion.

Now Joseph, it is fair to say, is young and strong, bright and intelligent. He has muscles where Potiphar's have lost their definition and turned loose and saggy. He has a sparkle in his eyes where Potiphar's have glazed over with greed. He has energy where Potiphar has turned into a sloth and where no stirring in his bed is made except to fill his sluggish greed between his snores.

Is there any wonder my eyes have drifted to the hired help?

I have tried to be subtle in showing my affections to Joseph, but at first I thought he just hadn't noticed them. Soon I realised he was actually ignoring them and trying to be faithful to his master. It was very admirable of him, but I wasn't prepared to take no for an answer; I had my sights set on him and it was fast growing into an infatuation.

It is fair to say that I am not an unattractive woman: my legs are still slender and my curves (although wider in the hips than in my youth) are still tempting enough for any young man - I have seen many of the slaves and nobles alike glance at my cleavage or second glance at my rear as I pass by, but never Joseph.

I have tried with make-up and experimented with new hair do's to entice him, but still he pretends not to notice. I have even been direct with him. "Come to bed with me," I commanded him, but he refused. He said his master had entrusted everything into his care and withheld nothing from him except his wife and therefore could do no such thing as sin against God in such a way. Day after day I have gone to him begging him to relent his obedience to Potiphar and to his god, but still he resists.

Joseph is there now in the house alone. I will go to him. I am determined to take him to my bed and I will not take no for an answer, and I think it is fair to say that he will at last concede to my will, if he knows what's good for him.

Potiphar:

I've never felt so angry and betrayed before in my life! At first I thought it was a joke, thinking they had colluded together a tale for sport under my wife's direction. I know she's been bored of late so the idea of her fantasising some fabrication to pass her time in an attempt to grab my attention (admittedly I have been quite lapse at seeing to her needs of late) wasn't quite beyond the realms of imagination. I only took stock of their words when I saw the bitter hate in my wife's eyes and the eager expression of her servant girl who nodded profusely her support of her witnessing of the screams of her mistress, and then of course there was the cowering fear in the eyes of Joseph himself as he submitted himself to the restraint of the other servants of the house. Maybe if he had been restrained more forcibly my instincts of the crime would have been sparked more urgently, but he was boxed in by the stable hands with whom Joseph had the kindness and respect and whom felt little need to bind their charge who was dutifully awaiting my presence so he could plead his case.

To begin with my wife ranted and raved so that I could scarce make out a word she said. The tale unravelled itself in this manner: Joseph had entered the house and upon finding it empty of all but my dear wife then proceeded to tempt her to the bedroom. My wife being of honourable and honest disposition refused his charms admirably but the scoundrel refused to take no for an answer and grabbed my poor frightened wife with the intention of being forceful with her, at which point she screamed and he, not expecting that response fled the house.

Now I know Joseph is as handsome as I was in my youth and that he could probably take to bed any of the girls of his class (being a slave of course) and may even entice such noble of women with a polite gesture and kind word with that enigmatic glint in his eye, but my wife was, and is, and always will be out of bounds to him or anyone else. I trusted that slave with all I had and he returns my leniency and favour by treating me with such disrespect!

I don't know how many times I tried to question whether it was all a joke. Surely Joseph wouldn't do such a thing! But the near tears of my good wife were convincing, and then her anger began to turn on me for being reluctant with my judgement, accusing me of taking the word of a mere slave against the word of my own wife. I had no desire to dally in the argument then, and besides, there was the coat. Bare chested stood Joseph in his passionate yet flawed defence of his innocence in the matter as my wife stood there defiantly holding up the cloak she'd torn from his back as he ran from the house as she defended herself with her screams to alert help. Again the servant girl nodded profusely in support of the account, although, stuttering, she admitted not to have actually witnessed the whole event, but could testify to enough to satisfy a court if need be.

No court would be necessary to conclude the matter. I will not have my slave or any other, no matter how privileged they believe their position, making sport of their master's property or family. A message has to be sent to the slaves that this behaviour is not acceptable, and my wife will have her revenge or I'll never hear the end of it. I know a place suitable for such men as Joseph, a place beneath the city where the sunlight fails to pierce and where the smell of the city sewers is stifling, where one meal a day is fortunate if the jailer is in a kindly mood. It's not a place that receives visitors and none but those that command the royal guard have a key. Seldom does anyone pay interest to those incarcerated in the king's cells, for most who go there under the king's command never return to see the light of an Egyptian day again. It is a fitting place for the slave to rot till the end of his days.

The Cupbearer:

I told him not to do it but the fool insisted that Pharaoh would see the funny side. I said quite categorically that he would not and refused to help but, of course, knowing what he was up to I turned a blind eye. If only I'd been more loyal to Pharaoh than to my friend then maybe I wouldn't be here now stuck in this mess. Just a little wine, he said, maybe a little beer in the bowl. Oh, why didn't I stop him? You're probably wondering what it is I'm on about as I sit here in the dark dank dungeon of the royal prison. I've lost count now of the days we've been here; it's been more than weeks, but months only a few, I think. Anyhow, the baker and I haven't been here half as long as young Joseph. That young lad is a true nobleman! For a slave at any rate. I'm not quite sure what he did to get put in here but he's been here long enough for the guards to pretty much trust him with the running of the place. He's a friendly enough chap who never has anything bad to say about anyone and he faithfully does what the warden tells him, and so the guards pretty much leave him alone to get on with things. Not that there is much to do down here, but what there is to do is organised and routine as Joseph rallies round us and keeps our spirits up. I'd say he's got the respect of everyone down here, guards and prisoners alike.

Sorry, I went off track a bit there, I think I was telling you about the prank the baker and I pulled on Pharaoh. Well I say the baker and I but it was all his doing really, I just didn't stop him nor warn Pharaoh what was going on, which is why he chucked me down here with him. You see I'm Pharaoh's chief cupbearer, a kind of royal butler responsible for ensuring the king's cup is always filled, and trusted to ensure that its contents are never poisoned. Often I would have to drink of Pharaoh's cup, risking my own life when the king suspected foul play. It is an honoured position as few are trusted so completely by the king.

Now, Pharaoh loves his pets; he has cats and dogs that roam about the palace at their will, but at mealtimes his beloved hound, Abu, would forever dine at his master's feet. The baker hated this dog with a passion ever since it had made its way into his bakery and defiled his bread one morning. The king's breakfast having been spoilt the baker was held responsible and no blame could be apportioned to the trusty pet. I had thought this encounter had long been buried and forgotten by my friend and that his latest dalliance in practical joking, for which he is known at times to be a deviant master, was simply the latest in a long line of misplaced windups and attempts at getting Pharaoh to laugh and see him as more than just a baker. Of course, looking back on it now I can see that it was probably a little more than just an attempt to correct his master's misconception of his character and more an attempt at revenge at the proud beast that sat lapping the feet of the king.

Just a little wine, he said, just a little beer. I thought it was just that, a little. A little mixed in with the mutt's water to see how the brute dog reacted. An uncomfortable snort of the snout was all I expected. How was I to know he had filled the bowl completely with white wine and soaked the bread and meat in beer? I shook my head in disapproval when I saw old baker slipping away from the table having placed the dog's meal. I should have spoken up then, if I had then only the baker would be here now and I would still be serving at Pharaoh's table.

The dog went berserk of course. I don't suppose you've ever seen a large golden brown hound with a strong stature suddenly lose control, its legs turn to jelly, its ears go floppy and its mouth sags so that its tongue lolls out through a mouthful of slobber. I don't suppose you've seen a dog act like that, but if you have seen a man do the same then you know that being drunk is no good thing and they are incapable of controlling what they do. Such was with Abu as he slid about the floor and chomped unsuccessfully at nearby limbs. Fortunately the dog was able to be subdued without any harm coming to it, or to anyone else. Poor Abu, I did feel sorry for the poor thing. Needless to say that Pharaoh failed to see the funny side. I imagine that had it happened to someone else he may have been amused, but to see his Abu taken advantage of in such a way displeased him greatly.

Immediately I was questioned as to the contents of the dog's bowl and how someone had come so close to interfering with the king's meal. Everything on the table was tested and I was soon forced to admit that I knew who the culprit was, and that in my defence I hadn't spoken up in thinking no actual harm was meant. Unfortunately, in his anger, Pharaoh didn't quite see it that way.

So now you know how I got to be here sitting in these esteemed royal chambers with my fellow prisoner the baker, and Joseph as trusted keeper of our cell.

"You two don't look so good," said Joseph as he checked on us this morning. He was right, neither of us were quite ourselves. We were both preoccupied in our thoughts of what had disturbed our sleep as the fresh images that plagued us replayed on our minds.

"We both had dreams in the night," I said, "but neither of us understand them and there is no one here to interpret them."

This was one of the many hardships of being locked away in a prison cell. Not only did you have no access to

18

all that you owned, and missed out on all the comforts of home and being able to go about as you pleased, but you were also deprived of your friends and those that you would normally turn to for advice. If we had a dream in the palace then there were plenty of royal advisers we could turn to to try and tell us what the dream meant, and no one thought it strange to ask of such odd images, especially if the images felt so real as though they had meaning.

We both, as we told each other our dreams of the night, thought that our dreams meant something, we sensed it, but neither of us had the wisdom to unravel them.

"Do not interpretations belong to God? Tell me your dreams," replied Joseph.

One thing you need to know about Joseph is that he is a Hebrew slave who believes in this one god. It's not really the sort of thing that goes down well topside with the ruling class, but down here you have to kind of accept it; for one thing Joe, for a prisoner, has done well for himself down here and his god does seem to bless everything he does.

I thought, what have I got to lose? So I told him my dream:

"In my dream I saw a vine in front of me, and on the vine were three branches. As soon as it budded, it blossomed, and its clusters ripened into grapes. Pharaoh's cup was in my hand, and I took the grapes, squeezed them into Pharaoh's cup and put the cup in his hand."

I sat there waiting. I didn't expect Joe to be able to come up with anything clever or anything that the baker and I hadn't already thought of, but after a few minutes thought he took a deep breath and said, "This is what it means. The three branches are three days. Within three days Pharaoh will lift up your head and restore you to your position, and you will put Pharaoh's cup in his hand, just as you used to do when you were his cupbearer."

I took a gulp at the news, daring to hope that his interpretation could be true. There is little to hope for in prison other than freedom so the slightest glimmer of hope you tend to cling to with all your heart even though the chances of Joe being right were so far out there I couldn't calculate the odds. I half scoffed in embarrassment at the slight joyous smile I'd cracked but he just looked at me full of confidence and said in a pleading tone, "When all goes well with you, remember me to Pharaoh and get me out of this prison. For I was forcibly carried off from the land of the Hebrews, and even here I have done nothing to deserve being in a dungeon."

I nodded sincerely to him for this was probably the first time I had seen his suffering as an unjustly condemned man.

The Baker:

It's been a few days since I told him my dream just as my friend had, hopeful of a favourable interpretation as Joe crouched to listen to my account. He was all smiles as I began, seemingly enjoying the opportunity to flex what was clearly a gift he had at having interpreted the first dream so swiftly. My dream was all about one of my passions: food, so I was confident that Joe would have something good to say.

"On my head were three baskets of bread," I said. Joe nodded and smiled, knowing I enjoyed my role as baker and longed to be reinstated just like my colleague beside me. "In the top basket were all kinds of baked goods for Pharaoh." I could see my cell mate licking his lips out of the corner of my eye as he sat beside me. The food down here is far from adequate; it's tasteless gruel and in short supply and it's prepared in such unsanitary conditions there's no wonder we've all often fallen ill and been left to clean up our own mess (I won't go into too much detail but you can imagine the smell down here in an enclosed space with no ventilation when one of us is ill!) - oh how I long to cook up a feast back in my own kitchen! At times I drift off comforted by tricking my senses with the memory of the smell of freshly baked bread, but then I wake and breathe in and choke on the stale stagnant air and clutch at my shrinking girth.

Back to the dream. I apologise; food so often distracts my thoughts down here, especially when there is a lack of it. Joe sat there waiting, aware my thoughts lingered on the food itself, his hands raised palms upward and eyes widened as if asking for me to give him the rest of the dream, knowing somehow that it was incomplete. "That was it," I said, "there is nothing else, except for the birds at the end that were eating out of the basket on my head."

The smile faltered from Joe's face and his hands lowered with his eyes. He stood slowly and with a downcast and solemn expression looked from me to my friend and then back again as if not knowing how to break the news of what he thought my dream meant.

"What's wrong?" I asked him, but he didn't answer, not straight away. "Joseph?"

"I am sorry my friend, but this is what your dream means, at least what I think it means. Of course I could be wrong." He seemed to be stalling his explanation and suddenly I felt a sinking in the pit of my stomach as the walls around me closed in ever tighter and the air began to suffocate me. Instinctively I knew what he was about to say and I was about to tell him to stop and not say it, but I was too slow as he began his interpretation with his eyes thoughtfully looking to one side as if watching future events he was seeing in his head.

"The three baskets are three days. Within three days Pharaoh will lift off your head and hang you on a tree, and the birds will eat away your flesh."

Well as you can imagine there was a long uncomfortable silence after Joseph had said this. The cupbearer put his hand on my shoulder to comfort me as Joe silently slipped from the cell to give me some space to take in his message.

I've had a few days to think upon it now. At first I didn't get why I would be condemned and my friend would be freed. I reasoned that Joe was wrong and that he was talking rubbish. I have come to realise it is all my own stupid fault that I am here and had I been in Pharaoh's position maybe I would have done the same. I should apologise, and I will if he gives me the opportunity, but I know my king is unrelenting and unmerciful.

You know, sometimes I don't know whether it's always a good thing being able to know the future. Had I not been told I would have sat in my cell in ignorance thinking (or hoping) the guard at the gate now was coming to fetch me to the palace to be reinstated, but I know different and have brooded over this moment for the past three days since I told Joseph my dream. The turnkey is here now, I guess this is it.

The Cupbearer:

It was Pharaoh's birthday the day we were released from our cell, both the baker and I were led from the dungeons to be presented to his majesty at the feast. We were scrubbed down first of course; no one, not even newly released prisoners are presented to the king in an uncleanly state. I did believe, as did the baker, that Joseph was wrong and that we were both free.

We knelt before the king and he raised both our heads by placing the tip of his sceptre beneath our chins. I was quick to mutter a short apology for my actions, as did the baker, although his was longer and more rambling in his rehearsed speech; I guess following what Joe had said he'd had a chance to do some soul searching and had truly seen the error of his ways and had had the time to prepare his thoughts into words.

Pharaoh seemed pleased as he smiled with a tilted head in acceptance of the words uttered. He was, it seemed, in a good mood, it being his birthday. He signaled for an attendant and one came swiftly holding a pre-filled cup which was offered before me. I took it, remembering Joe's words about my dream, I smelt it and then took a sip. The wine smelt and tasted better than anything I have ever tasted before in my life; it's funny how captivity can heighten the senses and make you appreciate the finer things you previously took for granted. I waited a moment. There were no untoward effects. Satisfied it was not poisoned I then offered it to the king. He clapped his hands joyfully and then took the cup from me and urged me to follow him into the banquet hall where I could already smell the feast that had been laid out. As Pharaoh stood, he motioned for the guards to come forward and with a dismissive gesture bid them dispose of my friend the baker.

I didn't see him as he was led out. My last view of him alive was of his head bowed in disappointment, a tear streaking his cheek.

Through the window of the banqueting hall, where now I serve regularly, I could see amongst the day's festivities the gallows set up in the courtyard for Pharaoh's pleasure. An execution had taken place as entertainment for his birthday, and there I could see the baker's body swaying slightly as a bird swooped down to the gallows to perch at his head.

It's been a full two years since I've given any thought to my old friend Joe and my promise to him. There has never really been an opportune moment to bring up the subject with Pharaoh. I know it might sound bad, after all

I did tell Joe I would speak up for him, but really broaching the subject of a Hebrew slave in his dungeon that he doesn't even know is there and trying to convince him that he has been wrongly detained is much harder than I initially expected it to be. I admit I have been scared to speak up and put myself back in Pharaoh's bad books, which I would be, if it appeared I was trying to get a convicted prisoner freed, and a slave at that, and really why would Pharaoh care about him?

I have not forgotten my friend the baker and his body swinging outside the window; the image has served as a frequent reminder as to why to stay on Pharaoh's good side and do my duty diligently.

Today I have been reminded of my days of incarceration in the dungeon as the royal palace is a whirlwind of activity as magicians and wise men have been sent for and paraded before the king with great urgency. I've not heard the details of the dream but the word whispered amongst us servants is that Pharaoh had a nightmare that has disturbed him greatly and he wants to know what it means. From what I've been told no one so far has been able to interpret it and satisfy Pharaoh's unrest.

If I have found any favour with Pharaoh at all then I hope later today at his evening meal to remind him of the time when he was displeased with me and had me put in the dungeon, I think he will remember the incident because of the baker being hung on his birthday. I hope then, if the opportunity arises and the magicians have still failed to tell Pharaoh about his dream, to fulfill my promise to Joe and explain to Pharaoh how in the cells of the captain of the guard there is a Hebrew slave who successfully interpreted our dreams. Maybe then the king will send for him and Joe will get a brief taste of fresh air and a change of scenery for a short while before he is condemned back down to his cell. I will of course plead his case that he is innocent and not deserving of the sentence, having committed no crime, but alas I am not hopeful that he will be spared any mercy, but then as I remember, his god did seem to bless him in most things.

The Captain of the Guard:

They woke me late last night, admittedly I should have been up tending to my charge but instead they caught me dosing at my post. I was on the night shift you see; nothing much happens on the night shift. At night in the dungeon it is no darker than normal but still they sleep in a regular routine to keep them well balanced and healthy; it's one of the patterns that Joseph got all the prisoners doing to help keep their spirits up and their minds working so that they don't lose hope. He's a real treasure that lad. We all love him. We rarely have any trouble down there with him in the cells. If it wasn't for him I'd be up all night trying to get all the restless prisoners quietened down instead of getting my forty winks like everyone else.

As I was saying, they woke me up with a command from Pharaoh himself. Apparently he wanted to see the prisoner named Joseph, a Hebrew slave. Most of us down here call him Joe, yet no one really knows why he's being held; there's no record of his trial or sentencing, although I do recall that Potiphar had one of his slaves thrown down here a few years back for some rumoured indiscretion with his wife.

It takes a good couple of hours to get a prisoner looking respectable enough to be presented at the royal court; they have to be scrubbed clean and their hair cut and fitting clothes found. It can be quite an effort to get some of these guys ready, and with Joseph it took most of the night.

Breakfast came and went so Joseph was treated to his first topside meal in years; not bad to get fed the palace food whilst still in chains. Pharaoh wanted to see him after breakfast as he apparently had some wise men to consult with and if they told him what he wanted to know then I was to escort my prisoner back to his cell. As it was our wise men clearly weren't all they were cracked up to be as we were led into the king's throne room.

I have to say Joseph scrubbed up well and looked a darn sight better than me as I stood next to him. We both respectfully bowed to the king, Joseph not losing an air of grace or dignity as he acted as a loyal subject no lower than any of the royal court. Pharaoh nodded in a bow of acceptance of those stood before him and then began to speak.

"I had a dream, and no one can interpret it. But I have heard it said that when you hear a dream you can interpret it."

Joseph shook his head and I thought for a moment he was going to foolishly refuse, but then he said, "I cannot do it, but God will give Pharaoh the answer he desires."

Ok, here's where I admit to being a bit of a dumb guard, 'cause you see I thought at this point he was refusing and I was going to be ordered to run him through with my sword, which I really didn't want to have to do, 'cause really I like Joe. My eyes were wide with alarm and my hand was instinctively rising to my belt to the grip of my sword. It was only when Pharaoh proceeded to explain his dream that I realised that Joe wasn't refusing but was saying that he could interpret it if his god gave him the meaning. I relaxed a little then, quite relieved I can tell you, thinking to myself this was why I'd make a lousy king.

"In my dream," Pharaoh said, "I was standing on the bank of the Nile, when out of the river there came up seven fat cows and they grazed among the reeds. After them seven skinny and really ugly looking cows came up, the most foul looking beasts that I have ever laid eyes on in the whole of Egypt. The lean ugly cows then ate up the seven fat cows, not that you'd have been able to tell because they were still as skinny as before. Then I woke up."

Pharaoh paused but it was clear he hadn't finished. We waited for him to resume.

"I drifted off again and then fell into another dream. In my dream I saw seven heads of grain, full and good, growing on a single stalk. After them, seven other heads sprouted, withered and thin and scorched by the east wind. The thin heads of grain swallowed up the seven good heads. I told this to the magicians, but none of them could explain it to me, but you come highly recommended Joseph, so do you think you can tell me what all the wise men of Egypt cannot?"

Joe dipped his head in thought, or prayer, I couldn't tell which, then he looked up and said to Pharaoh, "The dreams of Pharaoh are one and the same. God has revealed to Pharaoh what he is about to do. The seven good cows are seven years, and the seven good heads of grain are seven years; it is one and the same dream. The seven lean, ugly cows that came up afterward are seven years, and so are the seven worthless heads of grain scorched by the east wind: they are seven years of famine. God has shown Pharaoh what he is about to do. Seven years of great abundance are coming throughout the land of Egypt, but seven years of famine will follow them. Then all the abundance in Egypt will be forgotten, and the famine will ravage the land. The abundance in the land will not be remembered, because the famine that follows it will be so severe. The reason the dream was given to Pharaoh in two forms is that the matter has been firmly decided by God, and God will do it soon."

Pharaoh looked mightily disturbed by the news as Joe recounted it and I was sure that the order was going to be given to execute the slave for predicting such dire news.

At the very least I thought he would be sent back to the depths of the dungeon to live out his days in darkness, but before Pharaoh could respond Joe, with great boldness, spoke up some more.

"And now let Pharaoh look for a discerning and wise man and put him in charge of the land of Egypt. Let Pharaoh appoint commissioners over the land to take a fifth of the harvest of Egypt during the seven years of abundance. They should collect all the food of these good years that are coming and store up the grain under the authority of Pharaoh, to be kept in the cities for food. This food should be held in reserve for the country, to be used during the seven years of famine that will come upon Egypt, so that the country may not be ruined by the famine."

I have to say that all of us present were bowled over by the wisdom that came out of Joseph's mouth for what he said made perfect sense, and the best part was that even if Joe was wrong Pharaoh had nothing to lose by following his advice.

I don't think any of us present had ever heard a slave speak so confidently to the king before, nor speak so wisely. None of us knew how the king would react; the situation was unprecedented.

We all leaned forward with breath held waiting for Pharaoh to utter a word of command as he sat motionless as if a molded statue of gold.

Slowly Pharaoh's head nodded and his eyes scoured the room looking at every individual. There were members of his royal household, royal officials and advisers, soldiers and servants and many people Pharaoh trusted to help him rule his kingdom. His eyes rested on none for more than a moment until they finally fell on Joseph, and there they stayed as he asked, "Can we find any-one like this man, one in whom is the spirit of God?"

No one answered. Pharaoh seemed to be giving credit to this foreign god and attributing Joseph's wisdom to this god, and what was more he seemed to be stating that this wisdom was greater than any found in Egypt. I'm sure none in the room agreed that this was true but then I doubted any wanted to contradict the conclusion of the king, so all remained silent as Pharaoh once again looked around the room daring anyone to answer. If anyone had a better solution than Joe then they didn't speak up. Joe had pretty much nailed it.

Then Pharaoh said to Joseph, "Since God has made all this known to you, there is no one so discerning and wise as you. You shall be in charge of my palace, and all my people are to submit to your orders. Only with respect to the throne will I be greater than you."

There was a murmur of disapproval which fell silent at the sharp rising of the king's head. No one could believe what they were hearing and many for days afterwards were questioning whether the king had gone mad, some even were rumoured to be considering overthrowing the throne and ousting Pharaoh from power. Pharaoh called for all his officials within days and put them all straight about his wishes concerning Joseph and threatened them all that anyone who didn't respect his new ruling regarding Joseph would be executed. Those loyal to the king helped identify those who wished to overthrow him and a good number of royal subjects soon found themselves with me as their lord and master as they were granted a stay at the royal one star guest house beneath the city as they traded places with Joe. If Joe had still been a prisoner they may have fared better in their captivity, but alas they were left alone to argue amongst themselves and drift into the insanity that often befell desperate prisoners who protested their innocence, claiming to be hard done by and plotting their escape and revenge.

The Herald of Zaphenath-Paneah:

Who am I? You may ask. I wasn't there when Pharaoh our king took off his signet ring and put it on my master, nor when he dressed him in fine robes of linen and put a gold chain around his neck. Nor was I there when Pharaoh gave to my master Asenath, daughter of Potiphera, the priest of On, to be his wife.

I came into my master's service in the years of plenty, when the food stores were high and the land was rich and fertile; back in the days when Pharaoh himself would ride with my master by his side in a golden chariot commanding all bow down before his appointed number two of all the land, to whom we were all to bow.

I was employed in those early years when my master, who at thirty was almost double my age, had already been given the keys to this great land and had already begun traversing the desert towns storing up the grain that was grown in abundance, storing it in the cities till our store houses were overflowing.

I bore witness to the birth of his children, the two boys, Manasseh and Ephraim, who as infants were too young to know that their father, the great leader of the nation of Egypt, besides Pharaoh himself, my master Zaphenath-Paneah, had once been a foreign slave held prisoner in the royal dungeon, and who had gone by the name of Joseph.

My job was for all to know his new name, for the name of Zaphenath-Paneah to be yelled out before the crowds so that they all knew who he was as he approached, so that they would all bow before him as I shouted at the top of my voice, "Make way!"

I was barely a man when I entered my master's service when the land was plush with fruit and the markets bustling and the people merry with the satisfaction of their harvests. It is true that in those early days there had been some discontent at the confiscation and the heavy tax of produce imposed by my master, but it was short lived as the people got used to it, and eventually it died out completely as we neared the foretold seventh year predicted by the royal court.

Just as predicted the seven years of famine began and the people slowly started to see firsthand the wisdom of my master as their crops failed and their own stores ran dry. It didn't take long for my role to change as I was no longer required to call out my master's name but instead was required to list the names in the queue of those begging for a hand out from the royal stores. The people went to Pharaoh as soon as supplies began to run short, but the king just sent everyone to my master, this was after all, his long term plan for Egypt's survival. Graciously, and fairly, my master controlled the steady release of food, ensuring that no one starved and no one was fed too much. The fat grew lean but no one in the land died of hunger.

In a very short time the famine had spread throughout the land and beyond our borders into neighbouring lands so that people from all over Egypt and the surrounding countries came to buy grain from my master. Pharaoh was pleased that his people had enough and that his coffers were growing fat at the expense of the hungry. The people were happy because there was food to be bought at a time when there should have been none, and also because they had forewarning that it might happen so had saved enough for the extra purchases (buying back their own grain from the king at a fair discount as arranged by my master).

Most of all my master, Zaphenath-Paneah, was happy because his god was being faithful to his word and was fulfilling everything he had predicted.

Jacob:

Must we die like this? Starving in our own land, wasting away, and forced to slaughter the last of our livestock to serve our families just one more meal. Eeking it out, and hoping it will last until the Lord provides a miracle to rescue us from our desperation.

I lift my hands up and bow my head low as I beg my Lord for mercy, for I know he can provide. I beg my God to forgive me and my family for our sins, for all the things we have done wrong, and to look with favour on us once again.

Day after day I get down on my knees in the dust of Canaan, no easy task now that my joints are riddled with the swollen stiffness of age, and once down I need the firm support of my boys to haul me up again. Not that they are boys any longer. Grown men my eleven lads are now, with families of their own, plowing the land of their inheritance. Not that the land returns any crop nowadays. There is no grass for the sheep. The ground is too dry and solid for the weakened oxen to plough. The wells have dried up. Bandits and thieves roam across the land prepared to carry off anything they consider worthy of earning them another meal. For this reason we huddle together in our great community, for there is safety in numbers, and they all look to me for reassurance.

And where do I look? To my sons who are to lead after me, for my days are drifting by like tumble weed blown by the wind. I have travelled far and journeyed long and soon I will strike the dry dead stump of a tree or the immovable boulder and I will come to rest, then my people will look to Reuben, and to Simeon, and to Levi, and Judah, they will look to Issachar and Zebulun, to Dan and Naphtali, Gad and Asher, and to Benjamin. But my sons are lacking in inspiration and leadership. I hate to admit it, but they are weak.

"Why do you look to each other?" I have asked them. If I, with dull of hearing, have heard that there is grain in Egypt then surely they too must have heard this. What are they waiting for? Must I command them in everything? Very well then, even in this I must take charge and direct them. If I don't send them then we are all likely to die here.

We have money enough to buy grain but they must be careful not to be robbed. Maybe the rulers of Egypt will be sympathetic to us starving Hebrews and take pity on us. I cannot, however, bear to lose them all. Benjamin shall stay behind. He shall be my comfort should I grow too weak before the others return, or should they fail to return at all. The youngest of my boys and the only glimmer I have left of my beautiful Rachel. He looks much like his brother Joseph and reminds me so much of the young man that he had grown to before he was snatched from me by that wild beast. I could not bear it if I allowed Benjamin to go and harm should come to him. I could not stand to lose the second of Rachel's sons.

The Servant of Zaphenath-Paneah:

I can't tell you how much I love my job. My master is so kind and fair. His family treat me really well and I almost feel as though I am related to them. It's weird, but Zaph (he lets me call him that these days) never looks down on me the way I've seen other slave owners do. There is a real peace in his house and he has the most devoted of staff, me included, who would bend over backwards to please him. To think, when I first started working for my master as his herald he was only a few years older than I am now. I don't know what it is exactly but there is a kind of connection between us, as if he knows what it is to be in my shoes, a young slave just wanting to do the best he can for his master. He has trusted me with lots of different tasks over the years and has confided in me in the briefest of detail that he was not born into this role but is from a faraway land and of a much humbler beginning. He told me once that he was then known by some as Joe, but he insisted that I wasn't to repeat it to anyone. I can't tell you how honoured I felt to be taken into his confidence and to be trusted with such a great secret. Often when we are at the royal palace he will give me a wink and pull a face at his discomfort at the royal ceremony or the constriction of his head piece. He has a great sense of humour, and as bosses go he is the best. If he wasn't my master and I his personal servant I think we would be great friends.

You're probably wondering why I'm telling you all this, eh? Well it's so that you get an idea of the looks passing between Zaph and I this morning as we stood vetting and calling out the day's visitors seeking food aid from my master, the governor of the land. I didn't know these men, I had never seen them before, but even before I called out their names I could see the change of expression on my master's face as he recognised the group of ten Hebrews from Canaan, brothers they claimed to be, seeking grain to purchase to take back to their people.

"Where do you come from?" I witnessed my master ask as he regained his composure and pretended not to know the men.

Not knowing what game my master was playing I carried on with my duties of attendance at his side as he took a keener interest in this group than he would ordinarily. For reasons of his own he hid his identity, which I surmised was easily concealed behind the makeup and gold necklace and head piece. I knew enough of his past to know he hailed most likely from the same region as these men, yet I had no way of knowing if they were friend or foe.

Seeing clearly after some brief conversation about where they were from and their purpose that they were ignorant of knowing who it was they were talking to, Zaph sharply and angrily blurted out, "You are spies! You have come to see where our land is unprotected."

I have to say at this point I still had no idea whether this was to be in jest or whether these men were actually dangerous so I simply just played along following my master's lead.

They protested vehemently, stating that they were honest men and all the sons of one man. But my master was having none of it, insisting that they were spies. Still they protested, and in their desperation they admitted to being ten of eleven brothers. So where was the eleventh? Zaph demanded. At home with their father they claimed.

My master leaned to me and whispered in my ear an instruction and so at his command I gestured for guards to be made ready to detain the ten men and hold them in custody. The soldiers circled the men as Zaph stood on a raised platform staring down at the proceedings, patiently waiting for the travellers to see the futility of resisting his might. When the brothers' anger and resistance reduced to fear they turned as one in submission as they waited for my master to speak.

"Here is how you will prove to me that you are not spies. I will give you time to choose one of your company to go back to your homeland and return with the last of your brothers. The rest of you will remain in custody here where your words will be tested by varying means." A fearful shudder ran through the group as they trembled at the thought of torture which danced tormentingly across their minds. "Failure to return with this other brother will result in... well let's just say an uncomfortable position for those that remain in Egypt, and a harsh lesson will be learned about the business of spying in our land."

If my master was playing a joke it did seem indeed to be a rather harsh and cruel one and completely out of character for my master, therefore I had every reason to assume that these men were indeed a real threat. I ensured that the soldiers bound each one carefully and then had them led down to the prison cells.

Simeon:

For three days we sat in that cell arguing between ourselves, distraught at the turn of events and each blaming the other for our incarceration. Which one will go? we asked ourselves. Three days we sweated our panic in the hot cells beneath the city. For three days I protested my innocence as Reuben pointed the finger at me, well not at me specifically, but I felt it the most I think as he blamed the whole thing as comeback for what we'd done to Joseph all those years ago. It wasn't the first time we'd argued like this. We all felt bad for what we'd done to our younger brother and we all regretted it and each of us in our own way carried our secret guilt on our sleeve. Dad still didn't know the truth so didn't understand the stupor we all fell into whenever something bad happened, paralysing our thoughts and emotions, crippling us with our guilt. We blamed the whole famine as payback for what we had done, and dad sending us to Egypt with our tails between our legs begging as a sign of this being true, as it was to Egypt that we'd sold the boy.

Our three days captivity came to an end when the lord of the land who had imprisoned us, Zaphenath-Paneah, came down to the cell with an apparent change of heart about keeping us all locked up, saving us from making the awful decision of who to send back, for none of us wanted to be left behind and none of us wanted to be separated from the others.

Zaphenath-Paneah was escorted down by an interpreter and his servant, the one who had us bound and imprisoned. All three stood there at the bars as we fell silent in their presence and waited for what would be said.

"Do this and you will live, for I fear God," spoke up Zaphenath-Paneah as he looked down his nose at us, "if you are honest men, let one of your brothers stay here in prison, while the rest of you go and take grain back for your starving households. But you must bring your youngest brother to me, so that your words may be verified and that you may not die."

At this our hearts were lightened as we could see that this lord was indeed wise and also fair, for in this way our families would get fed.

We turned to each other knowing we couldn't deny the offer of release for all but one of us and that convincing our father to allow us to return to Egypt with Benjamin was going to be a hard task in itself. It would all break our father's heart as he would risk losing the one left behind or all if he sent us all back at this ruler's command.

We said to one another once again, "Surely this is for what we did to our brother Joseph!"

Reuben replied, "Didn't I tell you not to sin against the boy? But you wouldn't listen! Now we must give an accounting for his blood."

Zaphenath-Paneah turned away, presumably fed up of our arguing between ourselves in a language he didn't understand, for we spoke in our own tongue. I gave a slight sneer to him over that which was caught by his servant. It was a foolish mistake which was to seal my fate.

The Servant of Zaphenath-Paneah:

I watched with interest the exasperated and desperate exclamations of the ten men stood uncomfortably in the cell, each in a contorted spasm of frustration as their body language screamed their urgency to be released as they pulled at their hair and their clothes, raking their beards with grubby elongated finger nails.

I'd seen it all before. These weren't the first I'd observed imprisoned in the cells. Few escaped an early term but the sentence served was usually just. On many an occasion the judgement of my master was more than lenient as he impacted a lesson learnt on the prisoner and then earned their respect and loyalty by awarding a fair trial and sentence.

I didn't understand their language and our interpreter echoed back their speech in broken Egyptian as Zaph pretended not to understand them. I could make out the name of Joseph spoken a couple of times and wondered whether this was in reference to Zaph and whether they recognised him. As the interpretation came back I realised two things: yes, it was to Zaph that they were referring, but not because they recognised him. This was confirmed by my master as he turned his back on them, his eyes welling with emotion as it became clear to me that these men were his very own brothers who thought that he was long dead.

With Zaph's back now turned I observed one of the group to sneer at my master. Whether it was his frustration or anger at his situation I wasn't sure; it was a natural reaction that one in captivity was prone to give his captor so I was not surprised. I alerted my master to the reaction for it would not favour my master to have his back turned to a potential enemy and it would serve him well to turn and show strength.

Zaph nodded his thanks to me and then muttered an order to me to secure the man who had sneered and to release the others from the cell.

And so it was that the one named Simeon was kept in prison on his own, the decision made that he would be the one to stay behind. The others were ordered by Zaph, via the interpreter, to return home and return as soon as possible with their youngest brother to prove they were not spies, failure to do so would see the death of Simeon in his cell.

The men were led away from the cells by the prison guards and held in the blindingly dusty courtyard while their donkeys were prepared for their journey back to Canaan. Their donkey's, however, were a while in coming for Zaph had set me a task with them before the nine men could leave.

Reuben:

The journey was hard going in the heat but we made good time, spurred on by our eagerness to make things right and have Simeon released. If we hesitated it was only at the thought of breaking the news to the old man, but our sense of doing what was right overrode our fear and so we hurried with all urgency towards Canaan. I'd be lying if I didn't have a niggling fear that the Egyptians would chase after us, having changed their minds about letting us go, but as we talked between us we reassured each other that Zaphenath-Paneah seemed a fair and honest leader, even if he had misjudged us and our intentions.

We stopped for the night close to the southern marshes of Lake Menzaleh as we passed stealthily through Goshen, each of us wanting to go on through the night but knowing that our donkeys wouldn't last the strain and needed to rest. We unsaddled them of their load and watered them and reached to our sacks to feed them. As a good will gesture the servants of Zaphenah-Paneah, at his command, had filled our sacks with grain to last the journey, paid for from our silver, which turned out was more than enough for us to take back the excess home to our father, and true to his word there was plenty for our families too. It was as we delved deep into our sacks, our hands reaching in the unseen darkness that we discovered something troubling. With a trembling hand I held out what tottered at the mouth of my sack and raised my voice above the others to be heard. "My silver has been returned," I said, "here it is in my sack."

We, all nine, stood still as the multitude of possible implications span through our heads. If the silver had been returned by mistake then we were likely to be accused of stealing it back. The Egyptians were known for their dislike of us Hebrews so we were clear in our minds that it had not been placed there through any act of kindness; it was this deep distrust and hatred of us as a race that underpinned the belief that we were spies in the first place. No good could come of this. We argued about turning back immediately with the silver but the words of Zaphenath-Peneah were quite clear, "Do not return without your younger brother!"

We resolved to set off early as soon as it was light enough to travel, collectively set in our minds that we could return the silver when we came back with Benjamin.

Each of us slept poorly that night haunted by the trial God had set before us and questioning where it would lead.

Benjamin:

"No! My son will not go down there with you. His brother is dead and he is the only one left. If harm comes to him on the journey you are taking, you will bring my grey head down to the grave in sorrow."

Dad gripped my arm so tight it hurt. The way he spoke to Reuben you wouldn't have thought that any of them were my brothers. I didn't fear the trip, if anything I was excited by the idea. I've felt so stifled here at home, constantly under the watchful eye of my father who has become so over protective of me over the years, fearing that harm will come to me any time I wander off from the village. Besides, I trusted Reuben and the others; they always look out for me and are always kind and caring towards me. Judah had even promised to take personal responsibility of me if I was allowed to go, and they all agreed they would not return for grain for our people without me. So I felt totally assured and at no point thought that they would purposely lead me towards harm, so confident was I that they would do anything in their power to protect me. I couldn't ask for a better set of brothers!

I know my father's reaction towards keeping me safe is purely out of his grief over what happened to Joseph all those years ago, but truly I want an adventure - I'd quite welcome a little danger at the hands of the Egyptian's far away from the confines of my own people.

I did all I could to side with Reuben as he put across his argument on behalf of them all, but the more I spoke the firmer the grip pulled me to my dad's fearful frame.

"Father," Reuben argued, "the grain we have will only last a short time. The only way of getting more is to return. And I will not lose another brother to Egypt!" He paused as though he'd spoken out of turn and whipped his head round to the others who were uncomfortably grimacing and looking purposefully away. Reuben recomposed himself. "I will not lose another brother," he said confidently. "We will return and rescue Simeon. Father, not only does the life of your son depend on this but also your reputation. They accuse us of being dishonest spies, if we do not prove ourselves none from this land will be able to seek mercy from the Egyptians. If this famine continues all our people will starve, Benjamin included! We must return and we must take Benjamin! Father, please!"

All fell silent. Dad's face was still stern and scowling at Reuben but I could feel his grip slowly loosening and knew Reuben's words had made an impact.

I'd never heard Reuben stand up to my dad with such authority, it was as if he had finally come into his own as the elder son ready to take his position in place of our father. I think dad saw this too. Reuben had left for Egypt cowering and fearful but had encountered a problem that brought out the best in him, and he was rising to his responsibility.

Dad released his grip and looked kindly to me, then gently he pushed me forward into Reuben's care. It was my coming of age, my dad finally saying I could be a man and leave the security of his protection.

I stepped towards Reuben and joined the others just behind him. Reuben was looking at me curiously, and then even more curiously at the others before returning to gaze upon our father. "Father," he said gently, "There are things you don't know, things I should have told you years ago but have been too scared to speak up. When we return I will tell you the truth and face your judgement and beg your forgiveness, but for now I must do what I can to restore our family."

At this a tear welled up in the eye of my dad, my father, the great man Jacob, Israel, the leader of our people. Whatever it was that Reuben was keeping secret my father seemed to have an inkling of it. He smiled a half smile and nodded, stepping forward he put his hand on Reuben's shoulder, then embraced him before turning and silently walking off. It was a poignant moment, so full of meaning. Nothing more was said and without delay we began our journey back to Egypt.

Reuben:

We arrived before the court of Zaphenath-Paneah and were led forward to answer with a matter of urgency as we were announced as the brothers from Canaan. We stood in a line, our sacks unloaded from our donkeys held before us. I stepped forward and boldly spoke the words I'd memorised and rehearsed, words that my father had entrusted me with before we left: "O ruler of a great people, please have mercy on my family and see them for what they are, eleven brothers and my sons. Do not take them for spies but for men caring for the interests of their father and his people. We are of no threat to Egypt. The famine is still severe in the land and the grain you had provided we have already used up. I have instructed my son to come to you with gifts of some of the best products of our land: a little balm and a little honey, some spices and myrrh, some pistachio nuts and almonds. Also they return the silver which they mistakenly returned home with, and to this end you will find double the amount. Finally they come with the last of my sons, Benjamin. I am a God fearing man and pray that God will give you eyes for the truth and return my sons to me."

Then I continued in my own words, "We are Israelites, sons of our father Jacob who is called Israel because he has wrestled with God himself. Please accept our gifts." As I finished speaking I bowed low as my brothers brought their sacks forward one by one and joined me in bowing before Zaphenath-Paneah.

The mighty man before us looked from me to my brothers each in turn as they stepped forward. His eyes lingered on my youngest brother, Benjamin, and a strange expression swept over his face which he tried to hide as he turned to his servant and issued an instruction. If I was not mistaken I'd a have sworn he was smiling with delight at having us all captured together. Immediately my heart sank as I wondered with sinking fear whether I'd led my brothers straight into an Egyptian trap.

The Servant of Zaphenath-Paneah:

I was pleased to see the brothers return for my master's plan seemed to be playing out just as he had predicted, and ever since they had left for Canaan he had been nervously on edge and ever watchful for travellers passing through our land. Now he had a skip in his step and could barely contain his excitement as his face beamed from ear to ear at the news they had returned.

I saw the look on his face when he lingered his gaze upon the young man that was Benjamin, and in that moment I saw the resemblance. I doubt anyone else would have seen it for few people get to see my master without all his finery and make-up on, but I have seen him as I've attended him in his chambers and clearly noted the cut of his chin so similar to the thickly bearded slant that drew the line of the twelve men, but none more so than in Zaph and Benjamin, whose thin shadow of growth betrayed their likeness.

At Zaph's command I led the ten men to Zaph's family home and had them wait in the central chamber out of the sun. I took them water to wash their feet and refreshments for both themselves and their donkeys.

As we entered the house the oldest of them, Reuben, grabbed me by the arm earnestly, yet courteously, and said, "Please my lord, if you are to seize us and take our possessions and animals and put us in prison with our brother Simeon, then know we came down here the first time to buy food. But at the place where we stopped for the night we opened our sacks and each of us found his silver - the exact weight - in the mouth of his sack. So we have brought it back with us. We have also brought additional silver with us to buy food. We don't know who put our silver in our sacks."

I could see the fear in his eyes, in all their eyes as I awaited the translation from the interpreter stood to my side. I nodded my understanding as I turned to them all with my best reassuring face and said calmly, "It's all right. Don't be afraid. Your God, the God of your father, has given you treasure in your sacks; I received your silver. There was no mistake in it being returned to you. Rest here a while until my master comes. He has instructed me to slaughter an animal and prepare a meal, for you are all to join him for lunch here at noon. Now if you'll excuse me I will also go and fetch your brother, who has been well taken care of, so that he may also join you for your meal." I then bowed and left the room, feeling their astonished faces staring at my back.

Nothing of the likes had ever happened in this house and I could tell from the buzz of excitement that I felt, which was infectious from my master, that what was about to happen would change the dynamics of things around here. As I left the house, instructing some of the other servants about the meal, they too caught the breath of fresh air sweeping through as the unusual events unravelled before us.

Joseph:

To say that I'm nervous is an understatement. Behind that door are all my brothers. All of them! I should be angry with them for what they did to me, but I'm not. There is a flood of emotion running through me that I can't contain. I can't stop crying. There is a mixture of nerves and joy and... fear, yes fear. From what I've observed so far they have changed, but I need to be sure.

After all this time it finally all makes sense to me. For a while I was mad at them and upset at having been abandoned and treated so harshly by my brothers, but I relied on God to bring me through the tough trials I faced in this foreign land, and the more I relied on him the more he blessed me, continually being faithful throughout my captivity and hardship. I could have stayed mad at them as I mourned the loss of my dear father. I could have sought them out from my position of power here in Egypt and sought revenge. I could have sent word to my father that I was alive and well. But what would all that have achieved. God has used me here. He has saved the lives of these people through me in ensuring none of them starve, and people from foreign lands have flocked to my door seeking the same. Yes, God has used my pain and suffering to elevate me to a position of power to help others, my own family included.

I remember the dreams of my youth. I didn't understand them then, none of us did. The sheaves of wheat and the stars bowing down to mine. How arrogant I was about it at the time, no wonder they hated me so much. I see the bigger picture now; it was all for God's glory. It was God who ordained me to a position of power in Egypt, placing me at a time of need to help my own people. My father's people need feeding and I will be God's servant and feed them.

I don't know how they will react to seeing me. I'm sure none of them have recognised me. None of them suspect. This will be a total shock to them so I will have to choose my moment carefully.

Just one more test.

How long have I stood behind this door? If Pharaoh could see me now cowering behind my own door I'm sure he would be amused. Men of our stature don't cower behind doors from anyone - others cower from us. How long have I stood behind this door? I can smell the food that has been prepared but I can't tell if my stomach is doing cartwheels due to hunger or nerves, the latter I suspect. I can hear them growing restless inside. Ok, here goes.

What a fool I am! Look at me staring into the basin at my own reflection in the water as I wash the tears from my face. I just couldn't contain myself and had to bolt from the room. What must they be thinking of my behaviour?

They each seemed humble as they presented their gifts and bowed low before me. The dream: such fulfilment of what I dreamed so long ago. That in itself brought everything flooding back. Yet they still suspected nothing even when I asked about our father.

He is alive and well! My dad is alive and well!

It is a good job I was communicating through an interpreter otherwise they would tell the tremor in my voice and would maybe recognise my accent too readily.

Barely was I in the room when my eyes rested on Benjamin, my full blood brother, the younger son of my mother. I have missed the years we would have grown up together, but hopefully we can make up for lost time.

I pleaded ignorance when I saw him so as not to betray my emotions - fine how that worked out! "Is this your youngest brother, the one you told me about?" I tried to ask. "God be gracious to you, my son," was all I could blurt out before rushing from the room. I'm not even sure my interpreter caught my words fully.

What must they think?

I must compose myself and return. They must be hungry and no one can eat until I return. Take a deep breath Joe! Get yourself together!

The Servant of Zaphenath-Paneah:

"Serve the food!" my master commanded confidently as he re-entered the room. He gave me a reassuring nod to say that he was ok. Of all those present I think I was the only one who knew what he was wrestling with. I gave him a half smile and nod in return. He knew that if he needed to bale again from the room that I would cover for him and make excuses.

I jumped to organise everyone. There was protocol for the meal so I seated everyone in their set place as instructed. Zaph sat to one end to be served alone in a position where he could observe the whole room. The brothers were seated together in order of age, and the Egyptians who ate with my master were sat separately also. There were curious looks between the Egyptian's and the Hebrew's for they were not used to eating the same meal together, and to my countrymen it was detestable and dishonouring to be sat at my master's table in such a manner. If it were under any other master, even Pharaoh, there may have been more of a fuss made, but my master's guests knew he was intentional in most things so didn't grumble.

After a while there was much merriment as all those sat reclining for the meal began to relax and interact and enjoy the hospitality of my master.

There was a moment of amusement and bewilderment when the younger brother, Benjamin, was served five times the amount of the others. This was done at my master's bidding but none seemed to mind, indeed it became a poke of merry banter between the brothers as they rejoiced in his good fortune.

Before the meal finished my master beckoned me over unnoticed by the others and gave me instructions about the dismissal of the Hebrews. I was quite surprised by his commands but I kept the expression from rising to my face as I nodded in compliance of my orders. Zaph handed me his cup and I subtly drew it beneath my cloak so that, with my back turned, none of the others in the room could see. I then hurried from the room to prepare the sacks of grain for the brothers to return home with.

The brothers spent the day at the hospitality of the family as each of the brothers were introduced to Zaph's wife and children. I could see from the coy and reserved reactions of my master's wife that she was aware of who the brothers really were. Zaphenath-Paneah was very much a family man and kept little from his wife.

There is an annex wing of the house with guest bedrooms and so I prepared these rooms for our guests, for by the time the lunch meal was concluded the day was getting late and my master didn't think it fair to send them off so late and so clouded of mind, as they had consumed much wine from our cellars.

It wasn't until early the following day that the Hebrew brothers finally passed through the gates with their donkey's saddles loaded with grain for their journey home. They were in good spirits having feasted with my master and leisured under his hospitality, having earned his trust by adhering to his wishes in returning. It seemed a turning point in Egyptian/Hebrew relations as by the end of their stay even my master's Egyptian guests were conversing freely with the Hebrews.

In the morning they all parted with an embrace and my master jovially bowed his exit with excuses of having business to attend to.

I bid the brothers farewell and waved them off at the gate.

Then I waited.

Twenty minutes went by and still I stood watching the distance.

Forty minutes went by and I looked over my shoulder to the house to see Zaph step out onto the balcony of the upper floor. He nodded. I nodded back and then summoned the house guards to saddle the camels.

Camels can run fast when you need them to so it didn't take us long to catch up with the heavily burdened donkeys that were being led away with no particular urgency.

We caught up with the Hebrews who had been easy to track on their journey and surrounded them with menacing and unfriendly shouts. They looked terrified and confused as I indicated that they were to turn around and return to my master's house without delay. They complained begging a reason why, so I repeated what my master had commanded me to say: "Why have you re-paid good with evil? Which of you has stolen my master's cup, the cup my master drinks from and also uses for divination? This is a wicked thing you have done."

They all stood in stunned silence. They all knew of which cup I spoke; my master had drunk from this lavishly ornate cup the previous day and much had been made of its beauty and its purpose.

Reuben eventually stepped forward as spokesman for the rest.

"Why does my lord say such things? Far be it from your servants to do anything like that! We even brought back to you from the land of Canaan the silver we found inside the mouths of our sacks. So why would we steal silver or gold from your master's house? If any of your servants is found to have it, he will die, and the rest of us will become my lord's slaves."

I knew, of course, that one of them had the cup, but Reuben did not, so he had no idea of the gravity of his words and the consequences that would follow.

"Very well, then," I said, "let it be as you say. Whoever is found to have it will become my slave, the rest of you will be free from blame."

At this each of them, each assured of his own innocence, quickly lowered his sack to the ground and opened it. Then I proceeded to search their sacks, beginning with the oldest and ending with the youngest. They all watched with satisfaction on their faces that I had made a mistake as I began to empty the last of the sacks, but their smug faces didn't hold for long as the cup toppled out onto the sandy ground below.

All stared with mouths agape at Benjamin, yet none could match the surprise that read across the young man's face as he looked dumbly down at the silver cup at his feet and then confusedly to his brothers for help.

A couple of the brothers dropped to their knees in dismay, some tore their clothes and yelled out in frustration and anger.

Benjamin shook his head in denial, protesting his innocence.

I swear there were tears in the eyes of these eleven grown men, these brothers who stood devoted to one another despite the evidence that threatened to tear them apart once again.

I ordered them to repack their sacks and re-saddle their donkeys.

I have to say I felt sorry for them. They had been thrust back and forth by my master's games and had no idea as to the meaning of it all. They had no idea they were being tested. They had no idea that the hardship and trials were all testing their character and motives. I marched them back to the city scowling angrily at them as I acted out my role.

Judah:

We threw ourselves to the ground at Zaphenath-Paneah's feet as we entered his house. We all skidded on the floor in desperate servitude, pleading our innocence, knowing full well the penalty for our guilt. We begged for mercy and I remembered the promise I made to my father that I would personally take charge of Benjamin and ensure no harm came to him. It was at this moment I made up my mind that should it come to it I would sacrifice myself to free my brother.

The master stood before us scowling angrily, seemingly unable to speak at first his anger was so great, but then he cleared his throat and bellowed with a spite that silenced the whole hall so that even his servants took a step back: "What is this you have done? Don't you know that a man like me can find things out by divination?"

None of us dared lift our heads, but the silence that followed indicated that an answer was expected of us. I could sense the urge of my brothers wanting to tilt their heads at each other as none of us dared speak up out of fear. In the end, spurred on by my resolve to free my brother, I mumbled a reply to the dirt beneath my nose as I lay prostrate to the ground thinking of how I could save us from the death penalty. "What can we say to my lord? What can we say? How can we prove our innocence? God has uncovered your servants' guilt. We are now my lord's slaves - we ourselves and the one who was found to have the cup."

But the master said, "Far be it from me to do such a thing! I do not wish to make slaves of you all. No, only the man who was found to have the cup will become my slave. The rest of you, go back to your father in peace."

We all let out a breath and relaxed our bodies slightly as our eyes closed and in silent prayers of thankfulness to

God for sparing us. It must have been a sight to watch as I'm sure we all reacted in the same way yet none of us could see each other. Yet, as pleased as I was that the master wished to spare all our lives, I couldn't believe that Benjamin was guilty of the crime, and even if he were I had vowed to keep him safe. I lifted my head and saw the master staring at Benjamin who had raised his head in fear of his fate. The boy caught my movement and looked across to me with pleading in his eyes. Zaphenath-Paneah took a slow step towards him at which point I sprung to my feet before he could reach him and deflected his attention onto me. "Pardon your servant, my lord," I said, "let me speak a word to my lord. Do not be angry with your servant, though you are equal to Pharaoh himself. My lord asked his servants to bring our youngest brother here to Egypt which we did, but know that this was no easy task, for our young brother was born to our father in his old age and is the youngest of two sons born to his wife who is no longer alive. The older brother was lost to us many years ago and so our father was fearful of letting this one depart for fear that something would happen to him also. If we do not return with him it will destroy our father. So now, if the boy is not with us when I go back to your servant my father, and if my father, whose life is closely bound up with the boy's life, sees that the boy isn't there, he will die. Your servants will bring the grey head of our father down to the grave in sorrow. I personally guaranteed the boy's safety to my father. I said, 'if I do not bring him back to you, I will bear the blame before you, my father, all my life!' Now then, please let your servant remain here as my lord's slave in place of the boy, and let the boy return with his brothers. How can I go back to my father if the boy is not with me? No! Do not let me see the misery that would come on my father."

At this I bowed at the feet of this powerful man who held our fate in his hands; I even dared to grip his feet in surrender to him, hoping that he would accept me as his slave in place of my brother.

Desperate seconds passed into minutes as the sands of time fell slowly and silently, even the flapping wings of the flies had ceased to beat, and the ants paused their march, as with bated breath all raised a head in anticipation of the great man before us.

Joseph:

I held my breath. I could no longer keep this up. I could no longer control myself before all my attendants. My chin trembled as I slow counted to ten on my fingers just to give them some flex to distract from the uncomfortable unease of being still with all eyes on me waiting for my proclamation of judgement on my brother who had no idea what I was about to unveil to them.

I couldn't bear the eyes staring at me and it was then that I realised that this was no public affair. This was family. These were my brothers. I turned to my trusted servant behind me and yelled loud enough for all to hear so that there would be no misunderstanding of the command, "Have everyone leave my presence!"

No sooner was the word said than people started filtering from the room in hushed glances to each other. My trusted servant held back as he looked to me for further instruction. I gave him permission to leave with a tilt of my head to the door of my private quarters so that he knew I wanted him to stay close by should I call for him.

All that remained were the brothers themselves, all prostrate on the floor, Benjamin slightly forward, Judah by my feet. None dared to look up. The anger in my voice as I'd commanded the room was an act, but they weren't to know that yet.

What I said next I tried to say quietly and calmly but in my nervous excitement my voice rose too loud, so loud that all who had left the room could hear, not that I was aware of this until after when I was told that the word had spread and the Egyptian people were already gossiping about it.

"Brothers, look at me," I said in their language, already weeping as I bent down to them and raised each one from the ground with a gentleness they hadn't been expecting, "do you not know me? Look at me." I took off my headdress and tried to smear away the make-up with my tears. I don't know if it was the recognition of my face or of my voice as I spoke to them for the first time in our native tongue, but I saw a glimmer, a sparkle of confused familiarity dawn across all their faces.

"Yes my brothers, I am Joseph! Come close to me." Slowly and tentatively they edged closer and I grabbed each by the shoulder exclaiming loudly as I sobbed happily, "I am your brother Joseph, the one you sold into Egypt!"

I could see that they were still worried. Judah and Dan and Naphtali all looked to each other with that knowing look that said that their fates were sealed and that they were all dead men for sure. I jumped in quick to dispel the thought, "No, no, my brothers! Do not be distressed and do not be angry with yourselves for selling me here, because it was to save lives that God sent me ahead of you. For years now there has been famine in the land, and there will be more yet to come and there will be no plowing and reaping. But God sent me ahead of you to preserve for you a portion of what has been saved here by God's great hand.

"So then, it was not you who sent me here, but God. It was God who placed me before Pharaoh and made me lord of his entire household and ruler of all Egypt. Now hurry back to my father and say to him, 'this is what your son Joseph says: God has made me lord of all Egypt. Come down to me; don't delay. You shall live in the region of Goshen and be near me, you, your children and grandchildren, your flocks and herds, and all you have. I will provide for you there, because five years of famine are still to come. Otherwise you and your household and all who belong to you will become destitute.'"

Still they looked skeptical, but Benjamin's features were softening as he stared deep into my eyes. I returned the stare and smiled, and he smiled back.

"You can see for yourselves, and so can my brother Benjamin, that it is really I who am speaking to you." They all looked to the expression on Benjamin's face just before he embraced me. I held him tight for what seemed like an age and then drew strength to push him back at an arm's length, holding him by his upper arms and addressing the others: "Tell my father about all the honour accorded me in Egypt and about everything you have seen. And bring my father down here quickly."

What happened next was a dream come true as all my brothers rushed forward to embrace me and we all wept together and made our peace, and we talked long into the evening of all that had passed between us, and I asked eagerly for news of my father.

Pharaoh:

It's funny how good news travels fast. News reached me quickly although I think some of my servants were a bit hesitant in breaking it to me. Understandable really for the relationship with the Jews, an inferior foreign race, is not so straight forward or desirable to most within my kingdom.

But this news was of Joseph! Promoting him from the depths of a prison cell to command my kingdom was possibly the greatest and most rewarding decision I've made in the whole of my reign so far. Everything he has done has benefitted Egypt and its people and increased my standing as ruler. He alone, with his god, has kept Egypt in prosperity at a time when we could have floundered. Egypt could have been ruined by this drought and famine, but instead our neighbours have come begging to us for help. We are the centre of the world! And I rule!

So my servant's family have finally found him. Of course I knew this might happen someday. I had made it my business to enquire years ago as to how this Hebrew had ended up in my prison. Potiphar I had admonished over his abuse of power. Joseph himself had been quite candid with me about his background, having nothing to hide he had told me about his home and his love for his father and how his brothers had treated him. I had heard sob stories like this before of slaves and how they had come into service, but usually the slave's account was a miserable and desperate retelling in a bid for freedom, whereas Joseph from the outset had seemed content in being used in whatever position he seemed to find himself in, as if his god had placed him there for a purpose and he intended to live out his god's will.

Joseph's openness and honesty with me led me to trust in him, along with the fulfillment of the dreams which he had interpreted. In him I have found nothing to grumble about.

So when my servants told me of his reuniting with his brothers I sent for him immediately to ensure it was true and that it was indeed a peaceful and good union, for I knew it could be fraught with danger with these old rival brothers getting together after so long; it would not have surprised me if bad blood still brewed and daggers were drawn, but Joseph assured me all was not the case and that he was indeed a happy man.

I said to him, "Tell your brothers, 'Do this: Load your animals and return to the land of Canaan, and also take carts for your children and wives and bring your father and your families back here to Egypt. Do not worry about bringing your belongings with you for I will give you the best Egypt has to offer."

Joseph almost leapt for joy as I spoke the words, and bowing humbly he prayed a blessing over me, thanking his god for me. I have come to learn that a blessing from Joseph's god is worth much. What I did for his people I felt was the least I could do for him after he had saved my kingdom from disaster.

Reuben:

Before we left Joseph met us and furnished us with a great deal of provisions for the journey: new clothes, carts and donkeys loaded with grain and bread and other riches. For Benjamin he gave three hundred shekels of silver and five sets of clothes, but with this he gave a warning to the rest of us not to argue on the journey home. He looked at each of us, knowing the temptation to argue between ourselves over who was most favoured among us, over who had what and why, and over who was responsible for all that had happened. By his command he was reminding us of what had happened years ago between us all when we had betrayed our father and our brother by selling Joseph as a slave. Without hesitation we all promised to be good to each other on the journey home.

I looked at Benjamin and all the extra provisions he carried as we left and thought to myself that the old man would be pleased. My father would see the favour lavished on his youngest son, his favourite son, and would be happy in his old age. I hoped that when I explained to him about what we had done to Joseph all those years ago that he would go easy on us, especially when he saw the evidence that this was all part of God's plan. My father trusts in God, he himself has wrestled with God in person, so more than anyone he should understand the mysterious ways of our Lord. He who limps and has walked with a stick all these long years as a reminder of his encounter with the person of God cannot deny God's hand in what we have done, and how God has used his own son to rescue his people in these terrible times of famine.

Still, I am not looking forward to admitting the truth.

Jacob:

Well what a day this has turned out to be! Somebody pinch me, I'm sure this is all a dream!

Can my sons all be alive? Can it be true?

What the boys have told me has thrown my mind into a spin so that I fear that the diminishing mind of age has finally caught up with me.

Dear Reuben assures me it's the truth. The others cowered back as he stepped forward, chest puffed in forced bravery with Benjamin stood happily smiling at his side. I was so pleased to see my boy back safely.

Benjamin hugged me tightly and I could tell he was glad to be home with me. In his absence I had thought a lot about having held the reigns on him too tightly and I think the separation has done us both some good; it has been healthy for us.

Reuben bowed low as he came forward and I could tell immediately that there was news of grave importance to tell. My mind flitted back to what he had said before he left and so I braced myself for his admission of whatever guilty secret the boys had kept from me. Had it been just Reuben I could suspect any number of things, but it being all of them I knew it could only concern something of such gravity and collective guilt that, I surmised, it must involve whatever had happened to my beloved Joseph.

With shaky voice and shallow breath he told their guilty secret and then explained how Joseph was still alive and had risen to the giddy heights of being ruler of Egypt.

I thought it was all a joke at first of course, but Benjamin kept nodding his head and showing me fine clothes and silver, and the boys paraded the grain and donkeys and carts they had travelled back with. Benjamin pleaded with me not be harsh with his brothers for it was all ok, and Joseph himself begged for me to come to Egypt, and Pharaoh had agreed to allot us land to live in.

"Is it true? Dare I believe it?" I whispered to Benjamin.

Again he nodded, smiling with joyful tears in his eyes as he saw the smile edge upon my face, a smile so long absent. I lifted my eyes to the heavens and thanked my Lord. The stars were beginning to come out as the clouds parted in the twilight sky. The sun, moon and stars bowing down... I recalled his dream of so long ago. How foolish and proud I had thought it once, but now I could see it for what it was.

I looked down to Reuben and hugged him close, hugged them all close! My sons, all of them. God was fulfilling his promise to not let our people perish and die out. With tears in my eyes I said, "I am convinced! My son Joseph is still alive. I will go and see him before I die."

All that was earlier today and here I am lying in my bed still shaking my head in wonder at the great mystery of the ways of my God.

We have a long journey ahead of us. Hard as it is to leave this land, I don't suppose I shall ever set foot on its soil ever again.

It's a long tiring journey to Egypt and I'm not the young spritely man I used to be.

I did my fair share of travelling about when I was younger (albeit when I was fleeing from my brother's anger - I guess sibling rivalry has been part of our family for a while so I can't blame the boys too much as they know too well the stories of me and Esau and how I deceived my own father. Too many of their faults are my own.).

Ah, how this journey has given me much to reflect on as I sit on the back of the cart dreaming of the life I once had and the legacy I will leave behind in my sons. There is little left ahead of me now for I am too old to long for anything other than a good death and to see my Lord at the end of it. I have done all I can for my descendants - the next chapter must be theirs to live.

I was so scared by the time we'd reached Beersheba that I was hesitant in going on, but God spoke to me.

"Jacob! Jacob!" he called.

"Here I am," I answered. Hearing his voice was so soothing, so comforting to my mind, my heart, and my soul.

"I am God, the God of your father," he said. "Do not be afraid to go down to Egypt, for I will make you into a great nation there. I will go down to Egypt with you, and I will surely bring you back again. And Joseph's own hand will close your eyes."

A good death indeed. I know now what lays ahead, for my God has confirmed it. I will see my son again before I die and he will bury me in the land of my father before me.

We are the Israelites. This caravan of travellers. More than seventy of us: my family: my sons, their wives, their children, my grandchildren - my descendants.

We take with us all we possessed in the land of Canaan.

When we left Beersheba I was full of confidence, having met with my Lord.

I sent Judah ahead to seek direction to Goshen, the land that is to be our new home, and as I look out into the distance now I can see him coming, but he is not alone.

I see a prince riding on a chariot and my heart beats with excitement. Without hesitation I climb down from my cart and bow down to the ground in praise, and then, aided by my sons, I race to greet him. He is running now, and as he gets closer I can see his features. It is my son, the young dreamer now grown into a prince among men. He is embracing me, his arms wrapped round me, but I am numb with disbelief. I take a deep breath. Am I crying? Yes, my cheeks and beard are wet. I push him away. Look at him. Then pull him close. The embrace is now mine and I own it.

If only Rebecca could see you now my son!

"Now I am ready to die," I say to him, "with my own eyes I have seen you alive."

I cannot tell you how long we stood together like that, but I can assure you it was a long time.

PHARAOH'S BRICKY
(EXODUS 5)

Now I'm sure you've all heard the story about Moses, you know, the guy who as a baby floated down the River Nile in a basket and jamily was rescued by Pharaoh's daughter so that he grew up as a prince in the palace. What a touch that was, eh! Of course he threw it all away when he got older, that was when he caught one of us Israelite slaves taking a regular beating from an Egyptian.

It's common place for us that sort of thing, getting beaten; we work hard and do what we're told. It's a hard life, but we have no alternative so we tolerate it. Moses however, having grown up cushioned from the realities of how his adopted father in the palace treated us, his own people by birth, wasn't used to seeing the harshness of how we lived. Upon seeing an Israelite slave being beaten he quickly lost his rag and lashed out. I don't know whether he had intended to kill the Egyptian or not, but he did, then he tried to cover it up by hiding the body. Prince or no prince, killing an Egyptian in defence of a foreign slave was not likely to go down well back at the palace.

Of course all the workers back then knew what Moses had done. Word travels quickly amongst the workforce, and the guy that had been protected by Moses sought out help to hide himself for fear of any repercussions from the Egyptians.

Moses apparently came back the next day to check on things (personally I think he was trying make sure no one had discovered the body) but the labourers pulled him aside and told him what for, letting him know in no uncertain terms that he wasn't welcome: he didn't understand our people, he lived in the palace, and any attention he brought to our people was sure to be uncalled for.

Shortly after that Moses disappeared. It was rumoured he'd fled the country and the reach of Pharaoh, who was sure not to be happy with the un-regal behaviour of his adopted prince. The people said he lived out in the desert somewhere, but many of us thought he died long ago, disowned by everyone. That was until he reappeared.

It had been forty years since he had last troubled us here in the capital. We weren't exactly overjoyed to see him back. You see we're all hard workers, we have to be, we're slaves. There are a lot of us working tirelessly for Pharaoh who always seems to be coming up with building projects to keep us busy. The work is exhausting, packing bricks and leaving them out to bake in the sun and then transporting them to where they need to be, to then carry them and place them where the architects tell us. I usually have an idea of the building plans so I try to make sure all goes to the right building. It's heavy work and you've got to be strong for all the lifting, and there's no complaining about the backaches or being late in because we're too shattered or too sore to rise from our bed; whinging about the task is not generally tolerated by individuals.

Of course our people do more than just building work, but building is what I know; I'm a bricky. I make bricks and build houses - that's what I do. But that's not all that I do, you see I'm the foreman on site, one of the few Israelites trusted to organise things and ensure the smooth running of the people and the work so that the Egyptians don't have to be so heavy handed with us. I also act as shop steward, which is the union representative responsible as acting as go-between between us, the slaves, and the Egyptians, our masters. If the people have a grumble about working conditions they bring it to me. If the people have a grumble about the food allowance they bring it to me. If the people have a grumble about not being treated fairly they bring it to me. I in turn take it to the Egyptians in charge of our work detail and then nine times out of ten it gets ignored. Occasionally we might get a sympathetic response, because generally we get on alright with most of those guys, we do have to live alongside them after all. But mostly our requests get sent further up the chain of command and get lost in the echelons of royal decrees set up to keep us subdued and submissive to the new Pharaoh.

It seems every new Pharaoh has an even bigger ego than the last, and since the previous one died (the one that Moses had fled from) the latest one has proved to be no different. Ever since taking power he has set us to work tearing down old statues and buildings and having new ones set up in his honour, making sure that his name is recognised and worshiped throughout Egypt.

There we were getting on with life as normal, not a great life living in slavery you understand, but better the devil you know if you get my drift. We made things work the best we could, having abandoned the dreams of returning as a people to our homeland, a dream which had died with our ancestors whom we had descended from to become the twelve tribes of Israel, the descendants of the twelve sons of Jacob. Then all of a sudden that old trouble maker appears out of nowhere with his family, he just walks out of the desert and starts rocking the boat and making life difficult all over again.

Don't get me wrong, I got his intentions, well-meaning as they were, but I don't think he cared much for how his actions would affect us little people.

He had a bit of a job, from what I hear, convincing the elders of who he was and why he was here. It had been forty years since he'd set foot in the city so now he was an old man who was known mostly by reputation. He pulled some fancy tricks with a staff that turned into a snake, so

I'm told, in order to convince everyone that God had sent him to convince Pharaoh to let us leave Egypt.

Good luck with that one mate!

None of us thought he had any chance of succeeding in getting anywhere with talking to Pharaoh, even if Pharaoh took the care to hear him out; he hadn't exactly left the palace on good terms. We thought he would face a hard time and maybe a beating and then be put to work with the rest of us. We never thought it would come back to bite us where it hurts.

For days we forgot about Moses as we got on with our work; life moving on as normal. On the other side of the city I heard that some of the workers had downed tools as Moses got them all riled up about seeking permission from Pharaoh for all the Israelites to leave for three days to go and worship God in the wilderness. Needless to say it didn't go down well.

The next day our slave drivers didn't deliver the straw for making the bricks. The straw gets mixed with the mud, compacted and dried in blocks in the sun, the straw helps them to set in one piece and hold together and stay whole - we can't make bricks without the straw. Naturally I complained, or rather questioned where the straw was. With the slaves stood idle behind me I was told that from now on we would have to fetch our own straw. Great!

I sent the word round and we broke into details to go and fetch straw from the fields. As you can imagine it took a while before they returned and so our day of brick making didn't get going until nearly lunch, by which time we were already behind on our usual quota.

"Make sure they know we'll be down on the brick count today," one of my friends urged.

"Of course they know we'll be down today, I don't need to tell them," I responded.

The next day, still no straw. I organised another detail to fetch the straw. Another day down on brick supply.

The building work was beginning to slow as supply ran out.

At the end of the second day the slave drivers came to me aggressively arguing that we were down on production and demanded a reason why. I complained that we hadn't been given straw and had to collect our own and that was the cause of the delay. They didn't see it as an excuse for not meeting our quota of bricks so they did what slave drivers did best - they beat me.

The next day I called a union meeting with the other reps, having each of us consulted our slave members upon a course of action. The members urged us to go and appeal to Pharaoh, so that was exactly what we did.

I left my team of workers gathering straw and packing bricks as we marched defiantly up to the palace to demand an audience with Pharaoh.

Pharaoh made his thoughts quite clear. He called us lazy. Lazy for not meeting our quota. Lazy for wanting to shirk work by desiring to leave to worship God in the wilderness. There was no budging him. No straw, and produce the same number of bricks - or else!

There was no doubt about it, all this was Moses' fault. He had gone to Pharaoh requesting we be let go, and Pharaoh's reaction was to make us work harder and beat us more if we failed.

We left the palace and made a beeline straight for Moses and his mouthy brother Aaron who was with him. We moaned at them bitterly because of what they had done, which had made Pharaoh hate us even more and would now find any excuse to kill us if we stepped out of line.

Having vented my anger I left Moses and went back to my work detail and got on with my work. What else could I do? I had complained to the slave drivers. I had complained to Pharaoh. I had complained to Moses. All the complaining in the world wasn't going to change Pharaoh's decree. Who else was there to turn to?

To be fair to Moses he did look regretful at what had happened and genuinely seemed concerned that his actions had caused us so much trouble. Even as we left him I heard him fall to his knees behind me and cry out to the Lord for help. It was the one person I hadn't thought of lodging my complaint with.

I wonder if that help will ever come. I wonder what it would take to change Pharaoh's mind.

THE KING WHO GAVE IN
(2 SAMUEL 11&12)

King David:

This is where all my troubles started. If only I had joined the war effort once the rains had ended instead of kicking back and putting my feet up and watching the army, my army, marching off along the dried out and newly passable roads.

I could pretend that it was the first time that I'd noticed her, but really I was looking out for her. I guess that makes me a royal peeping tom. She was the real reason I stayed at home in the palace. She was the real reason I was willing to risk all to temptation: my kingdom, my honour, my family, my friendships, and my faithfulness to God. Yeah, I guess you could say I was being pretty stupid and wasn't really thinking straight, having been blinded by lust. I know, I'm a king and so should have known better, but I'm also just a man, and none of us are perfect.

So there I am lying in my bed one night, I couldn't sleep because I was waiting, waiting for her. Now from my bed chambers in the palace I have a fairly good view over the city, I can see most of the homes close by, most of which house my royal guard and servants. I can often look out and see what some of my servants are doing, not that I make a habit of it, not usually anyway. There are a few steps from my balcony which take me up to the roof where I occasionally like to stretch my legs at night if I can't sleep, usually when things are troubling me or I need to think out a campaign strategy. Very little is hidden from me here.

I had previously observed that things were tense between her and her husband; she resented him going off to war so often and they had argued on occasion about it. I could have intervened to help but it is a man's affair to manage his own household and mine to command my men to war when needed.

Her husband was away fighting, where I should have been. He should have been fighting at my side, defending me, his king, but in my dalliance at the window she had caught my eye, and I hers, and so to my chamber I remained, watchful for just a glimpse of her.

Don't be mistaken that this was the first time we had gazed at each other from our own private habitats. She had pretended not to notice me but our eyes had locked on more than one occasion as we appreciated each other's admiring glances. She would often step out to bathe when the light faded so as not to be noticed by anyone, other than me. She knew I watched, why else reveal so much and not hide from my downward gaze.

On this particular night I went up on to the roof and waited for her to appear, when she did she looked up, saw me, and smiled. She then proceeded to bathe herself. I couldn't contain myself. I felt exhilarated, excited beyond measure with a forbidden fantasy running through my head.

I rushed down to the balcony and out through my chambers to rouse my attendant. I brought him back through to the balcony, by this time the beautiful woman I had been observing was no longer in view. I pointed to where I had seen her and asked my attendant who lived there. I knew the answer of course but made at a pretence that I didn't know for I wished her to be fetched back to the palace without him knowing I had been watching her. He told me the woman of the house was called Bathsheba, "She is the daughter of Eliam and the wife of Uriah the Hittite," he said.

I made a gesture of recognition and nodded affirming that of course I should know who lived there. "I must speak with her, bring her here immediately," I replied.

She came soon after, willingly and without complaint. In the dark of night none but my closest attendant knew she had been summoned to the palace. She stayed the night in my chambers and left early in the morning without being seen.

As I looked down from my balcony in the light of the next day's dawn and watched her re-enter her family home a twinge of guilt suddenly struck my heart. She looked up to see me but I quickly retreated into the shadows of my room.

As much as I desired her I knew what I had done was wrong and knew I had to distance myself from her. Of course there was also the small matter of the law: to be caught in adultery invoked the death penalty for the guilty parties. If anyone were to find out that she, a married woman, had spent the night in the arms of the king then it could result in more than just a public scandal.

Call me callous, a typical man getting what he wants and then discarding it like a piece of trash, but that wasn't how I meant it to come across. I knew I couldn't afford to give in to the temptation again, if I did I was afraid it would soon lead to obsessing about her, and that was sure to ruin me.

Bathsheba:

It is shameful what I have done. I had slept in the bed of my king, I, a married woman. If my secret were to be discovered I could face being stoned to death for adultery. As for my king, I cannot comprehend the public disgrace he would face and the damage that it would do to his reputation.

I have kept my distance from the palace since that night, knowing that I can only go to my king at his request, but he has not sent for me since. I must go to him now, or at least send word to him, for now everything has changed.

My husband, Uriah, is away at war, and has been for many months, so I know my current condition is not due to him; there is no way he can be the father of the child I am carrying.

How will the king deal with the news that I am pregnant, and that he, the great King David, is the father?

Surely he also has much to lose by the news, so it would be in both our interests to try to cover over the scandal by bringing Uriah home from the field for a short period so that I can claim he is the father. I hoped that the king would read between the lines of my message as I sent word via my servant to the palace to tell the king that one of his most trusted soldiers was due to be a father.

Am I scared? On so many levels yes, yes, and yes! I've never been pregnant before, so that in itself is scary. My child is of royal blood, so that too is daunting. Not knowing how the king will react to the news and whether he will treat me favourably or whether he will treat me with distain and deny the sin we are embroiled in is terrifying. Despite what we have done, he is an honourable man, so I am hoping he will try to do good by me.

And then there is Uriah, oh how I have wronged him! My lies, my deceit, and my unfaithfulness to my husband will at best have him raising a child as his own who is not his own, or if not he will be dishonoured. Would he join in those condemning me? Would he cast the first stone? I don't know. In anger and shame and in the heat of passion men do strange and irrational things which they may later regret.

I am at the mercy of the men in my life, and I must face the consequences as they play out.

King David:

A message came to me, innocent enough to anyone not understanding its hidden meaning. A request underlined the words, or at least I read between the lines to quickly come up with a proposed plan of action.

When I received the message, which came to me via my attendant, who in turn had received it from Bathsheba's servant, I was by the kennels having taken my favourite dogs for a long walk across the fields. It was fortunate that when the word was delivered my head was bowed in attention to the dog licking at my palm. I'm sure my face quickly flushed upon hearing that Bathsheba was pregnant. My stomach grew heavy and my legs weak, conveniently I was able to sink to one knee to stroke the dog and suck in a breath as I absorbed the shock of the news.

"Uriah's wife?" I feigned surprise with an edge of uncertainty of whether I knew her or not. My attendant confirmed her identity as I hid my shame and anger at being placed in such a predicament. Fortunately the attendant that brought the news was different from the one who had brought her to the palace on that dark night when I gave in to temptation, so I was in no fear of him putting two and two together.

The truth of this couldn't come out. I had to somehow cover this up and quickly!

"It would not be good for Uriah to be absent from his wife at such a time as this. Send for him from the battle field, but don't send word as to why, tell him instead that I wish a brief account of the war effort. The news of the child should be hers to tell. Speak of it to no one, even after he has arrived back, they may decide to keep it a private matter until it becomes obvious she is with child. Uriah is a fine and loyal soldier, if I know him as I think I do he will be eager to return to the fighting until the child is born or the campaign is over, whichever be the sooner."

At this I dismissed my attendant and made my way to my chambers where I collapsed on my bed and cursed the open view from the balcony which had brought me such dread. I was overwhelmed with fear as to what might happen, but one thing I knew for certain: that I could have no contact with Bathsheba and could do nothing that could arise any suspicion to alert anyone that I had had any sort of relationship with Uriah's wife.

Uriah:

I was glad for a respite from waiting around with the men. The days are long and gruelling, ensuring all our forces are in the right positions to ensure the siege of Rabbah continues, making sure our men keep up with their training and maintain their high spirits as we worship the Lord in battle. God goes with us and the Ark sits at the centre of our camp ready to be carried to victory over God's enemies.

It is unusual to be called back to Jerusalem to report on the progress of the war effort, but then King David doesn't normally stay behind in the city. I'm sure he has his reasons for staying behind and it is not my place to question my king's motives.

My report to the king was brief: the majority of the Ammonites had been defeated during the fighting that had begun at the beginning of the campaign, many of our men were held back to secure the taken ground and secure the plunder and ensure the necessary offerings of thanks were presented to the Lord. The forces laying siege to the town of Rabbah were dug in for the long term but a swift end could be brought by a large scale assault, but it was likely to cost more of our own men. So far our loses were minimal and our gains great, I recommended to the king that we held our current position as there was no rush to end the war, except that was to demonstrate God's mighty hand in a swift crushing victory.

I humoured my king by telling him he was greatly missed and that progress may have been swifter if he was in the field. He was much flattered by this but showed also a hint of regret at not having joined us. I hoped he would say he would join me on my return but he made no sign of wishing to join the men. It was a shame, for the king to join the battlefield would have boosted moral amongst the troops and sent a shiver of fear across to our enemy, for they know God's hand goes with him in battle – he is still known as the David who slays tens of thousands.

Having delivered my report to the king he told me to go home and rest, to relax for the night and take time to spend with my wife. Admittedly the thought of going home and spending a night in my own bed was appealing, but things had been tense with Bathsheba when I left for war, and to be back for such a brief time could distract me too much and cause us to get into conversation that would play on my mind when I should be concentrating on war. I didn't want to argue with her about not being around to pander to her whims, and then have to leave after a brief night of passion. That in itself was against the king's commands: fighting men were not allowed to be with women during a campaign by order of King David himself, so his instruction did leave me half wondering whether he was testing me to see whether I would break my vow. Besides, how could I enjoy the comforts of home when my men were facing the hardships of the camp, guarding the presence of the Lord – I longed to be back there where God was present amongst our army.

I'm sure the king understood this, and no doubt longed to be there himself, but I'm sure whatever kept him away was important. He clearly missed it and asked after some of his favoured men, including our commander Joab.

I reassured him of all he asked and then, having been dismissed to go home with his blessing, I left his presence and went to spend the night at the palace entrance with the other palace servants. I decided it would just not be fair on either of us if I went home to Bathesheba; it would be better that she didn't know I had returned.

Bathsheba:

Who knocks at my door at this hour? It looks to be a messenger from the king. What can this mean? Don't react Beth. Just don't react to whatever it is.

What is this? A gift? From the palace? A platter of food from the king's table. I can't say that I'm that hungry, I ate a small meal earlier and there's no way I'll get through all this on my own.

The servant claimed it was for my husband and me, but I am here alone. Unless the king has sent for Uriah and he is here in Jerusalem. That would make sense. Ah, I think I see the king's plan.

Maybe Uriah has been delayed at the palace. I will make up our bed chamber and await his joining me there, hopefully he won't be too long.

King David:

I got up early. In truth I had slept little. On a couple of occasions through the night I wandered out onto the balcony and up onto the roof to peer across at Uriah's house. I saw no sign of life there. I just hoped Bathsheba knew her part and had taken him to her bed, if not then I would have to take more drastic measures.

It was these measures which I played over and over in my mind as I lay in my chambers spinning scenario after scenario around the tornado in my head. There were so many things that could go wrong that would bring about an undesirable outcome to their night together. I could picture them easily getting into an argument, as they have done on so many occasions, and he storming out, or she storming out, or she blurting out that she was pregnant in a fit of rage. But of course she wouldn't do that; she's not that foolish or impetuous. She knows the risks, and to give him any hint of her condition would be disastrous for her.

Lying awake I wrote a number of letters in my head of things I could put in place should Uriah return to the palace in the morning with things having gone sour. The anxiety was tearing at me and so I rose before the dawn and washed and dressed and made to walk with the dogs through the courtyard to clear my head.

I'd not gone far from my room when one of my attendants, who was up preparing my morning meal, greeted me. I casually asked him if Uriah, the Hittite, had come yet this morning to the palace from his home. My servant looked a little confused and embarrassed as he informed me that Uriah had not left the palace during the night but had instead slept with the other servants.

I'm sure my mouth hung open, a mixture of dismay and anger swirling within in a rising foaming tide.

I made my way to the palace entrance and sought out Uriah who was up already and helping some of the other servants with their early morning tasks. He is truly a gallant man and I can see the characteristics that drew Bathsheba to him in the first place. He is loyal and noble and does me great honour – much to my shame for what I have done to him in his absence and what I was yet to do to him.

I marched up to him and barked at him, in as friendly and as jovial a tone as I could muster, although I'm sure I failed in this and he felt more berated by my brash approach. "Uriah, haven't you just come from a distance? Why didn't you go home?"

His answer, yet again, put me to shame and I'm sure this time my face flushed scarlet.

"My king," he said bowing to me, "the ark and Israel and Judah are staying in tents, and my master Joab and my lord's men are camped in the open fields. How could I go to my house to eat and drink and lie with my wife? As surely as you live, I will not do such a thing!"

There are few such honourable men as he! At his words I felt a hammer of guilt strike my heart at my absence from the battle lines. But I had already committed a grave sin and I needed to cover it up; I needed to protect my secret.

My mind thought quickly, this was one scenario my mind hadn't planned on. It hadn't occurred to me that he wouldn't have gone home at all, I just assumed that any man given half a chance would have taken the opportunity of going home and indulging in the comforts of a good wife.

"Stay here one more day," I said to him, "and tomorrow I will send you back." I figured one more day during which I could convince him to go home to Bathsheba would be all that was needed to solve all my problems.

Uriah:

Aaarh! My head hurts so much! Never have I been so drunk as I was last night. The king was on good form and insisted I ate and drank with him most of the day as I had refused to go home to Bathsheba. He insisted I was a fool not to go home but I explained my reasons, the alcohol making my tongue a little looser than normal. I told him about some of the problems we've had in our marriage and how the war had made it difficult to maintain a healthy marriage. He seemed to understand; obviously he has been in the same position himself. Still, he insisted I go home, but I argued it would be too distracting from my duty and not fair on Bathsheba. He just laughed and plied me with more drink.

"Go home!" the king ordered as he turfed me out of the palace in the early evening. I felt it a real privilege to be honoured in the presence of the king. He dismissed any formalities as we enjoyed each other's company as friends. He is a great man, the king, and it is easy to see why so many follow him into battle. I hoped he would open up as to why he stayed behind during the current campaign but he didn't and I didn't feel I'd earned the position to question him on it. I lost track of the amount of wine we consumed, but I do remember enjoying myself.

"Go home to your wife!" he shouted after me as he pushed me towards the palace doors. I waved a casual hand back to him without trying to turn to look in his direction, I was sure that to do so would have left me stumbling and falling flat on my face before the king. I'm sure he would have laughed at that.

I walked out of the palace towards home but I didn't get far. I don't know whether it was just that I was too drunk to be sure of making it to the house, or fear of confronting my wife in my drunken state, or just feeling guilty that I had been drinking heavily with the king when the troops were still out in the field, either way I turned back and laid out my mat amongst my master's servants as I had done the night before.

*** *

79

Aaarh! My head hurts so much! Again! I think I drunk as much last night, if not more, than I did the night before. That's now two days and nights drinking in the company of the king. I am now so overwhelmed with guilt I cannot bear to stay any longer.

I should be in the field with my men, and with the ark. What will Bathsheba think if she finds out I've been here in the city these last few days and have not even graced the threshold of my own home or sent word to her? As for the king, I have to say I am a bit confused as to why he is going out of his way to entertain me so much. Maybe he is lonely and just wants the company of a fellow warrior, I'm not sure. I wish he would return to the battlefield with me for it would surely boost the men were he to ride in to seal the fate of the siege of Rabbah. What fear would shake that city then to know that the great King David was afoot! A surrender would surely be imminent.

The servants are all stirring now, and so too will the king be soon. I will go to him and insist he send me back to the battle and request he send word with me to encourage the men.

King David:

The words of the letter were written in my head way before the ink was set to paper. His loyalty will be his undoing, but that cannot be helped. His fate is sealed and he carries it now to his doom. I wish there were another way but I cannot afford for this scandal to come out. Those about me who would wish my crown for themselves would reach up to seize it; do not my own sons lay in wait for my demise? And they be my friends and family; there are other enemies still that would plot my downfall - that is the curse of royalty.

Then there is Bathsheba to think about. She would not likely survive the ridicule.

I sealed the letter and sent him off. Uriah was so eager to be on his way, he even begged me to go with him. I just shook my head and placed in his hands the letter with instructions to hand it to Joab, my trusted commander of my armies and my confidant. Uriah thought he carried with him words for the men to rally them and lift their spirits. Let him think so, he will never know the truth of what he carries.

Joab:

"Uriah! My dear man, what kept you? The king held you at his pleasure for far too long."

"Forgive me Joab, the king was indeed keen for my company. He gave me word in the form of a letter for you."

And so it was that I, Joab, received the letter. I read it with a stern and unflinching face that denied my true feeling of regret. I'm sure the king had his reasons, but mine was not to reason why. Orders were orders and I dared not question how Uriah had displeased my lord during his short visit to the royal city.

I dismissed Uriah and sent word of instruction for the men to lead a new assault on the city wall that was strongest against our forces. It made no sense to attack there; it is always best to attack at the weakest point not the strongest. We risked losing men in a pointless skirmish, but then that was the point. That was the order that saddened my heart.

I reread the letter to be certain of my lord's will, and then I burnt it.

Uriah:

Joab has not given any word to the men from the king so I can only assume that our new tactics today are on directions from the king based on my report to him. King David must see some advantage in this new attack or else he wouldn't command it, and he is a military leader of legend amongst the men so we all trust his judgement in these matters.

Some of our men are cowering back; they do not seem to have the confidence in our king as I do. The city wall is ahead and the enemy soldiers posted there have seen our approach and are making their way down to meet us across the field. They have a trench before the wall and archers up high to defend them so they are most difficult to get at. If all goes ill with them then they have the luxury of retreating beyond their own wall, but for us we are out in the open where they can rush at us and then run back to the safety of their defences and leave us to be fired upon from the archers above.

"Forward!"

Joab's shout bellows across the field and I run on command with my sword held high. We have the ark, we shall not die!

Their men leap out from their trench where they had lain hidden and there are more than I had expected. Yet more are coming from the wall.

I look to my men to spur them on but we are few, too few.

Had I missed a command to retreat? Where are our forces that had run up with me? I turn to look and see those I had relied upon scampering silently away from the battle like cowards. Behind me I hear the clamour and angry shouts of the enemy as they engage in us few left to fight. There is no time for flight, the enemy is upon us. I raise my sword and bat away a strike from the first man and then I crush him in the face with my elbow and I force him back to make room for a swing with my sword. I slice at one and then another, but to my right and left my men are falling. Needlessly we are perishing, losing the battle. The king has sent me to my doom, but I cannot fathom why, nor have I the time to think on it.

I see rather than sense the archers on the wall. They are picking us off from a distance. The few of us that are left try to shield ourselves by drawing close to the enemy footmen.

There are two about me now, no three. I know I won't be able to hold them off for long.

I try to glance back to Joab, hoping he is sending in reinforcements, but I cannot crane my neck to see and all my ears can hear are the cries of my men gurgling on their own blood as they fall to the ground.

I manage to strike one of my three opponents in the throat with my fist and he falls back allowing me to put my weight forward against the two swords interlocked into mine.

There is a small gap in my armour at the rear underside of each arm which in battle is rarely noticed. However if your enemy has the opportunity it can be taken advantage of should you be foolish enough to allow him to have an unchallenged approach to your back. This is not a predicament the armies of the mighty King David have ever had the worry of for we are all well prepared for battle and well trained: we fight in formation and guard our rear. Except on this occasion our rear guard had fled the battle scene.

As my third opponent regains his balance and charges forward once more the two swords unkink from mine and swing back in preparation for a further three pronged attack. I step back defensively and feel the sharp blade, so deviously encircled within my defences, pierce through the gap in my armour, its cold blade running deep within my chest and out through my sternum.

This is the end. I don't know why. The events of the last few days are absent from my mind. I fall to my knees, my eyes fixing on the ark I can see in my mind. It is still with us. Though I fall, our army will not.

Messenger:

"What is this?" the king demanded as I stood before him ready to present the account from Joab, the commander of the army at Rabbah. I am used to running back and forth from the field with messages, usually a call for more supplies or directions for reserve forces or carrying lists of the fallen, never before though have I been requested to deliver a message directly to the king himself.

I had to be quite persuasive with the palace guards before they would let me through under escort of King David's personal bodyguards. I know the protocols in addressing the king, just like in delivering any other message, it's what I'm trained in; it's my job. That doesn't mean I wasn't nervous standing before him. My hands shook and my voice held a weak nervous crackle as I recited the words Joab wished to convey.

When the King realised I was sent from Joab he seemed more eager to bear me in his presence. His face lost the hint of annoyance of being disturbed and took on an eagerly concerned frown.

I related the general details of the campaign and I could see the king's face begin to flush. "The men overpowered us and came out against us in the open, but we drove them back to the entrance of the city gate," I relayed. "Then the archers shot arrows at your servants from the wall, and some of the king's men died."

As I stood there his chest filled out and he clenched his teeth and his hands ready for an outburst of anger. I was ready for this. Joab had warned me the king would be angry that the army got so close to the city needlessly, where it would be obvious that they would pick off our men with arrows from the wall. Joab had pre-empted how the king would react and had given me a way of defusing his anger. I didn't know what it meant but I wasn't going to wait until I was shouted at before I said it. As soon as I saw the king's anger rise I blurted it out quickly and waited to see how he would react. "Also, your servant Uriah the Hittite is dead."

Immediately the king's face relaxed, a relieved smile sagging his cheeks. He nodded to himself and let out a deep sigh. Then he raised his head back towards me and said, "Say this to Joab: 'Don't let this upset you; the sword devours one as well as another. Press the attack against the city and destroy it.' Say this to encourage Joab."

With a nod of his head I was dismissed and escorted out of the palace by the bodyguards and sent straight back to Rabbah to deliver my new message.

I didn't know what that message meant at the time, but looking back on it now with all that has transpired since, and the gossip that filtered through the city, I know that King David wasn't as honourable as I had once believed.

Bathsheba:

This is what I get for my betrayal. I'm sure some will wonder why I'm crying after I've acted so dishonourably towards him. It's not tears of guilt that streak down my face. I did love him, he was my husband after all. I never wanted anything like this to happen. Why do men always have to go out to war? Why do they always have to fight? Uriah would still be alive today if it wasn't for all the conflicts David gets us into. I know it's not just his fault: he follows God into battle; it's him I should be blaming!

I don't know where I stand now. I'm a widow, who is going to look after me? Who is going to look after my baby?

At least Uriah was seen to have come home to Jerusalem so people will assume the child is his and I can avoid the scandal. His death it would seem has saved my life, but I've already heard whisper that he died because he came home to me, that he fell because he was distracted by his wife, going against the orders of the king to abstain during battle. If only they knew that I didn't see him, that he never came to my bed, and that he was the most honourable man that I have ever known.

The king has sent word that he wants me to live in the palace and care for me. I'm sure he is riddled with guilt at getting me pregnant and now without a husband to care for the baby. I know he liked Uriah and would have wanted the best for him, despite abusing that friendship whilst my husband was away.

The king wants to raise the child as his own. And why not? It is his after all, not that anyone else knows that. But what does that mean? Does that mean that he will marry me? He has other wives so another would not cause any controversy, if anything it would make him again the hero in the people's eyes as he takes in the wife and child of one of his fallen soldiers.

I cannot imagine God is pleased with any of this, but I am a subject of the king, whom the Lord has appointed over us, so I will again be obedient to his desires.

King David:

So I have told my story as to where all my troubles have begun. I make no excuses for my sin, for it is fair to say that I gave in to temptation and allowed my sin to overtake me in my zeal for my God.

This last year has been a hard one, but not because anything particularly bad has happened. My reign is secure. The kingdom is secure. The people are content. I am again a new father - Bathsheba has given me a son. Yet in all that has transpired I have been beside myself; a hole has emptied within my heart and lays vacant waiting to be filled.

We throw parties at the palace and I laugh and smile, but inwardly I am desperately sad. I spend time with my children and try to give them pointers on how to live their lives honouring God, but I feel a hypocrite riddled with regret grating the flesh beneath my skin. I lord my power over the people all the while expecting, even daring, someone to challenge my guilt. I lead the Lord's people in worship yet I can't seem to talk to Him myself.

How long has it been since I picked up my harp and sang a song to my Lord? How long has it been since I fell upon my knees in prayer and submission to my God? My guilt has built a wall between me and my God and I hide behind it, fearful of what he will say to me and how he will react. It is easier to bury my sin and hide from it than to confront it.

Nathan, my friend and counsellor came to me. I hadn't sent for him so I knew immediately that he had something on his mind of importance. He is a Godly man and the Lord speaks to him. When he came before me I was apprehensive. Part of me knew he was bringing God's judgment on me. Part of me welcomed it.

Nathan's face was stern; an angry tension tightened his cheeks. He proceeded with the usual pleasantries expected when coming into my presence, but when my attendants left the room his manner changed and immediately he launched into a story, giving me no opportunity to talk or interrupt. I stood with my head bowed and listened.

"There were two men in a certain town," he said, "one rich and the other poor. The rich man had a very large number of sheep and cattle, but the poor man had nothing except one little ewe lamb he had bought. He raised it, and it grew up with him and his children. It shared his food, drank from his cup and even slept in his arms. It was like a daughter to him. Now a traveller came to the rich man, but the rich man refrained from taking one of his own sheep or cattle to prepare a meal for the traveller who had come to him. Instead, he took the ewe lamb that belonged to the poor man and prepared it for the one who had come to him."

As Nathan told the story I grew angry at the injustice of the rich man in the story and quickly understood my friend's concern and why he'd brought this matter to me to pronounce judgment. "As surely as the Lord lives, the man who did this deserves to die! He must pay for that lamb four times over, because he did such a thing and had no pity."

Then Nathan replied, "You are the man!"

I looked at him with shock and confusion. What was he talking about? Then I realised he'd blindsided me with the story and that my original thoughts about his visit were correct. I took a step back, the blood draining from my face as Nathan stared me in the eyes and pronounced God's judgment upon me.

"This is what the Lord, the God of Israel, says: 'I anointed you king over Israel, and I delivered you from the hand of Saul. I gave your master's house to you, and your master's wives into your arms. I gave you the house of Israel and Judah. And if all this had been too little, I would have given you even more. Why did you despise the word of the LORD by doing what is evil in his eyes? You struck down Uriah the Hittite with the sword and took his wife to be your own. You killed him with the sword of the Ammonites. Now, therefore, the sword will never depart from your house, because you despised me and took the wife of Uriah the Hittite to be your own.'"

I felt sick to the stomach as Nathan spoke. No one knew, not for certain anyway, but Nathan spoke with absolute certainty and authority; there was no doubt God was speaking through him. I quickly thought back over the story he had told: Uriah's cherish lamb, Bathsheba, and I, the rich man, stealing her for my own selfish needs. How could I argue with the facts? My anger subsided and I put my hands out to accept whatever punishment Nathan would declare.

"This is what the Lord says: 'Out of your own household I am going to bring calamity upon you. Before your very eyes I will take your wives and give them to one who is close to you, and he will lie with your wives in broad daylight. You did it in secret, but I will do this thing in broad daylight before all Israel.' "

A tear began to roll down my cheek, a mixture of fear, regret, and relief, as I said to Nathan, "I have sinned against the Lord."

Nathan replied, "The Lord has taken away your sin. You are not going to die. But because by doing this you have made the enemies of the Lord show utter contempt, the son born to you will die."

I would have preferred it if he had said my life was forfeit rather than the child's. The baby was a child born of a sinful act, but still it was just a child. The sin was mine, it should be my life to be taken.

I slumped down onto a cushion and began to sob. I cared little that I did it in front of Nathan; my sin was uncovered and my family was about to be torn apart because of it. I had reason to cry and cared little at that point who was there to see it.

Nathan left. I didn't even note his departure. I remained in my chambers for sometime, I'm not sure how long but sometime later in the day a servant came with news that Bathsheba's child had fallen ill. It felt like a dagger to my heart as Nathan's words echoed in my mind.

I sent the servant away and bowed down to the ground on my knees, pleading with God to spare my son, begging him to have mercy and save the life of the boy. I knew there were consequences to sin but I never dreamt that what I had done would cost me the life of one of my children.

Over the next few days I left my chambers only to see the boy. He was a beautiful baby but he lay listless and still. His breathing was shallow and he wouldn't feed. Bathsheba too looked strained and fearful. She had commanded every known medicine to be brought to revive the boy but I knew none of it would be of any use, only God could save the boy now.

I locked myself in my room and fasted and prayed to God for the child, throwing off all comforts as I begged God to let my son live.

My close family and friends at the palace tried to get me to eat, even lifting me from the floor to get me to walk about, but I pushed them away. I didn't want their help. All I wanted was for God to change his mind and punish me, not the boy. I guess, thinking about it, the boy will never know the hardships of life but will know always the closeness of God, and his loss to me is punishment enough. Even as anointed king, who am I to question God's judgment?

The King's Servant:

For seven days my king had locked himself away, desperately praying for the baby to get well. It was on that seventh day that the child died.

We had all been worried about the king's health and his mood over the preceding days, but now our concern was how he would react to the news of the death. None of us servants wanted the job of breaking the news to him. We had all heard the wails of King David's wife, Bathsheba, as the boy stopped breathing in her arms. We all knew that David would not listen to anyone whilst he was praying for the child to live, now that he was dead we all thought the grief might overtake him and he would do something desperate. Men, even powerful ones, can do irrational things when emotion takes over. Every bad scenario we could think of went through our minds and we discussed them all amongst ourselves, trying to think of how we would handle each situation as it arose.

A few of us went up to his chambers having drawn the short straw to break the news. We stood outside the doorway whispering our hesitation about what words to use and how to actually break it to him. We stood too long at the door and didn't notice the king edge towards us. No doubt he had heard the cries throughout the household, for there were none who were not affected by the infant's death.

"Is the child dead?" he asked. "Yes," I replied with a dry rasp, wanting to elaborate with comforting words but in the moment simply adding, "he is dead."

Strangely and totally unexpectedly the King straightened up and demanded water to wash, and fresh clothes to wear. Quickly we darted about the chambers and attended to our lord's request, each of us awaiting an outburst of distraught emotion, but it didn't come. Instead he ordered we prepare him a meal whilst he went off to worship God.

We were confused and curious, boldly we asked, "Why are you acting this way? While the child was alive, you fasted and wept, but now that the child is dead, you get up and eat!"

He answered, "While the child was still alive, I fasted and wept. I thought, 'Who knows? The Lord may be gracious to me and let the child live.' But now that he is dead, why should I fast? Can I bring him back again? I will go to him, but he will not return to me."

Bathsheba:

David came to me shortly afterwards. He was different, not as distant as he had been before. I thought at first that maybe he was relieved that our child had died, but after talking with him I realised that, though he was deeply saddened by the death of our son, he was at peace once again with the Lord our God. My husband no longer has to hide his sin. We have both paid for our adultery, and the pain of losing my child will never leave me.

I think this might bring David and I closer together. He no longer sees me as the object that tempted him and drew him away from his Lord, but instead as his wife. He talked to me kindly and with compassion. He explained what Nathan had said to him, that God had taken our child and that David's family would turn against him, all as a result of how he had treated his servant, my husband Uriah.

My husband has gone off to war again. He joined Joab and has taken the city of Rabbah, where my Uriah fell, and he has taken the crown from the king of the Ammonites. When he returns I will tell him that I am pregnant again. This baby is conceived out of love and not lust, within a marriage instead of an illicit affair. I am scared for the future of David's family, and for myself, but I feel this baby will grow to do great things, so I pray that God will look kindly on this child.

A BOAT IN THE STORM
(JONAH 1)

The first time I met this clown I was just finishing up loading supplies down in the hold. Me and the rest of the lads had been busy prepping the ship ready to disembark. The deck was cleaned and cleared of the last of the crates and barrels which we'd lowered below. You can never really take enough stuff for a long voyage but there is only so much space on board and weight is always a concern.

Ours is a cargo vessel transporting goods for merchants from one port to another. Often the merchants themselves will travel below deck so that they can be there to unload their merchandise to start selling it immediately at the port markets at the other end. Occasionally, for the right price, we take on paying passengers who are wanting a speedy route to distant lands. This scrawny little guy who stood by the jetty looking our ship up and down from hull to mast was one of those wanting to board as a passenger.

You can tell the type: lost looking, enquiring eyes trying to figure out where the boat is going and whether the crew looked trustworthy, sometimes they look furtive as they flee whatever life they're leaving behind. This one was no different.

I stuck my head up out of the hatch and caught his eye as he placed his foot on one of the ropes binding us to the shore. A couple of the others had seen him too but as yet none had bothered to pay him any attention. If he was wanting passage he would have to ask, we had enough duties of our own to be getting on with to stop and give him the time of day.

"Where are you heading?" yelled across the man as I lifted my body out of the hole.

"Where are you wanting to go, friend?" I asked back, stepping over the edge of the boat and spitting into the sink between us.

"West," he replied, "Away from here, away from Joppa."

"Is Tarshish far enough for you?"

The man stood and thought for a moment. Tarshish was the edge of the world, the southernmost tip of Spain where the main shipping lane ended before the great ocean out west. It was a long journey that stretched the whole length of the Mediterranean from the north of Israel - it would work out as an expensive trip for him.

He turned his back to me as he checked his pockets and looked about the port at the other ships, very few of which were ready to depart, and those that were being fishing boats set for short journeys into the neighbouring waters.

When he turned back he said nothing but gave a cautious nod. I pointed over to the first mate to indicate who he needed to speak to to secure his passage and then went back to work. That was the last I saw of him that day and I thought no more of him as we got under way and set sail, heading south along Israel's coastline before following the Egyptian trade route out into the Mediterranean.

The beginning of our journey was calm enough, but that night the weather turned against us. We hadn't been prepared for the sudden burst of wind and rain that battered us; all the signs had been for a favourable start to our journey. All the passengers stayed below deck during the night as we fought with the wind and strapped down the ship against the waves that threatened to toss us and our goods aside to the watery graveyard about us.

For hours we battled the storm, and most of the passengers rose from their slumber as their stomachs hurled with the rise and fall of the ship. The captain, who at first had brushed off the storm as nothing of concern, was now panicking as we rocked to the very verge of being capsized. There was a real danger of the ship breaking up as the wooden masts began to crack under the strain.

The captain, desperate not to lose control of his business and the charge he was entrusted with, held out as long as possible before ordering the cargo to be thrown overboard to lighten the ship. You can imagine the protests from the merchants as their livelihood was fed to the sea to appease it, but even their cries of dissent were muted as they bore witness to the waves that threatened to rob them, not only of their goods, but of their lives.

I have to admit, I'd never seen a storm like it, and nor have I since.

Each of us on board fell into prayer, a cacophony of garbled cries as we each prayed to our own individual gods, hoping that one of them at least would be listening to us.

We huddled together below deck questioning each other as to why the gods were so angry with us and seemed determined to sink us. The captain went to rouse all those not present, finding only one of the passengers still asleep. The captain yelled at him, "How can you sleep? Get up and call on your god! Maybe he will take notice of us so that we will not perish."

The man looked shaken and a withdrawn unspoken tale of guilt lined his face. He looked even scrawnier in the dim light than he had looked when I had seen him stood next to the ship at Joppa.

We all sat together, convinced one of us on board must be to blame for our fate, and each picked a small stick to cast down in a pile on the floor to cast our lots. We wanted to know who had upset the gods and turned them against our voyage and this seemed to be the only way of discovering who was guilty. We let the sticks fall and our scrawny late passenger's turned up on top.

"Who are you? What is your name?" asked the captain. These were questions the first mate would already have asked when he boarded, but the captain probably hadn't cared for the details at that point so long as he got his fee.

"My name is Jonah, son of Amittai," he replied.

We then bombarded him with questions as to where he was from and what he was running from and why he had brought this calamity upon us.

He answered, "I am a Hebrew and I worship the Lord, the God of heaven, who made the sea and the dry land."

At this our hearts sank. Of course we knew of the power of the Hebrew god and the stories of what happened to people who went against him. We were terrified and so the first mate asked, "What have you done?"

"My Lord instructed me to go to Nineveh to speak to the people on his behalf, but I didn't want to give them his message, for he will rescue them from their sins and I don't want them saved."

"Nineveh is in the opposite direction to Tarshish," I stated.

"Yes, I wanted to get as far away from God and what he had called me to do as I could, but there is no escaping him, he is everywhere."

"You must really despise the people there," I said.

He lowered his head and nodded shamefully.

We knew we didn't have much time before the ship was beyond saving. The sea was getting rougher and rougher and the captain was looking as hopeless as the rest of us. "What should we do to you to make the sea calm down for us?" the captain asked.

Jonah, it seemed, had already been pondering this question as his response was immediate and assertive: "Pick me up and throw me into the sea," he replied, "and it will become calm. I know that it is my fault that this great storm has come upon you."

We all looked to each other. We were sailors not murders. None of us relished the thought of throwing a man overboard. Instead we took to the oars and began to row as hard as possible back towards land, but the more we rowed the harsher the storm grew against us.

Then we cried out to Jonah's god, "Please, Lord, if we throw this man overboard, don't hold us accountable for his death."

We took Jonah up top and reluctantly we lifted him over the side of the ship and threw him into the sea. The moment Jonah hit the water the winds calmed down and the waves subsided, and as I watched his body sink into the darkness of the sea, under the moonlight I saw what looked like the gaping mouth of a great fish swallow Jonah whole before sinking to the depths with its prize.

This should have been the end of my story, but it's not.

Our boat limped back to dry land, broken and battered, with no cargo, and with the captain and the ship's owners having suffered a hefty financial loss. As for me and the rest of the crew, we were now out of work. What was to be a good few months at sea had collapsed into a desperate scramble for employment. The ship would take a long time before it could be made seaworthy again. I settled in my mind to head back towards Joppa or maybe towards Gebal or Arvad beyond, knowing full well that no boats in Joppa were hiring. Maybe part of me knew going north along the coastal route took me along the path to Nineveh, the great city that Jonah was fleeing from, but most probably it was just coincidence that I should stumble across the strange tales as I moved north looking for work.

I got as far north as Sidon about a week later, that's when I first heard the rumours. People said that a ghostly waif of a figure had been seen wandering the road, his skin blistered and peeling. They said he looked in pain as he hobbled along mumbling that he had to get to Nineveh to deliver a message from God to the people there.

Initially I dismissed the story, but then I heard someone tell that they had seen a giant fish spew the man up onto land further down the coast. I thought back to that night when we had thrown Jonah overboard and the glimmer of the fish beneath the waves that had swallowed him whole. Then I wondered at what a couple of days in the belly of a fish might do to the human body, how the bile acids might blister and bleach the skin, and how Jonah himself had said there was no escaping God.

I felt sorry for Jonah, for if he was by some miracle still alive, and the stories I heard were of him, then his own prejudice of the people of Nineveh had resulted in a great deal of pain for himself, suffering for a message it seemed God was determined he deliver anyway. If he looked as bad as people claimed then the people of Nineveh would be foolish not to listen to what he had to say.

THE CALLING
(LUKE 5:1-11/JOHN 1:40-42)

To say I was tired would be an understatement. I'd been up all night and had caught nothing of worth, so as well as being tired I was also frustrated. All I wanted to do was get the nets sorted out and go home and climb into my bed for a couple of hours of well-earned sleep.

We had the nets stretched out across the boat, my brother, Andrew, had one end and I had the other as we both hunched over them, scrubbing them clean as swiftly as we could, both eager to get home. The boat was pulled up on the shore and our backs were to the land as we looked out to the selfish Lake Gennesaret which had refused to give up its spoils during the long night.

We heard the crowds coming before we saw them, they were a fair way off, coming onto the beach further down where the children usually bathed and the women washed the clothes. We stopped what we were doing for a moment as we took in what was happening and wondering whether we should join the crowds. Even from this distance we recognised Jesus. We had both met him before: Andrew had introduced me to him one day after he'd gone off with John to one of his baptising rallies down by the river. As they were listening to John preaching Jesus passed by and John had directed them all to him. Andrew left John that day and went off with Jesus. Andrew was so excited about his new friend that he ran home to fetch me so that I could meet him too. Straight away I could see why my brother was all in a fluster about this guy: he was totally captivating beyond words, and I'm not one for keeping my mouth shut. We got on really well with Jesus and by the end of the evening he looked at me and said, "You are Simon, son of John. You will be called Cephas."

A lot has happened in the short time that has passed since then. John, we hear on the grape vine has just been arrested and put in prison and so all his followers are on edge and trying to keep a low profile, Andrew included.

Jesus was drawing a fair crowd on the beach. Maybe people thought it was ok to stand and listen to him in John's absence. Maybe he was filling the void and silence left by the loud ripple that would usually stir across the hills and cut through the waters as John shouted his message of repentance to all who would listen. Whatever it was they were drawn to so early in the morning, word was spreading and the beach was filling up as the town emptied.

I had an inkling of what drew them. I'd sat captivated by his presence when I went to the place where he had been staying. For hours Andrew and I had talked about who this man was and what he was all about, we hadn't quite got to grips with his message but we loved just being with him.

I looked back to the nets, having satisfied my curiosity about the crowd, to see that Andrew was stood and waving over to Jesus off in the distance. I turned back again to see whether Jesus would recognise and remember us. As I turned the preacher was already walking towards us, talking to the crowd as they moved on mass behind him like sand being swept by the sea. He waved back to Andrew, and then to me.

Unsure I checked behind me, but yes it was me he was waving at. I raised an uncertain hand and stood, dropping the net as he drew closer. I was nervous. Had I not met him before maybe I wouldn't have been so daunted by him, but I knew he had a commanding authority about him which was hard to describe; he was a character you wanted to be close to at all times, but at the same time were fearful of, as though you didn't deserve to be stood in his presence. It was like being in the hall of a king, standing before his throne dumbstruck not knowing what to say. At least that's how I felt at the time.

As he drew near to our boat the crowd were pushing against him trying to catch his every word as he spoke. He turned his back to us and addressed the crowd by simply holding up his hand and they all fell silent. Turning back to us he smiled and climbed into the boat. Instinctively I jumped out and, along with Andrew, we pushed the boat back out into the water.

I nodded to James and John, our business partners who were in their own boat a short distance away from us washing their nets with their father Zebedee. They nodded back knowing we weren't planning on going out far.

We pushed the boat out a bit and then anchored down a little way out from the beach so that Jesus could address the crowd in comfort. Andrew and I sat back in the boat, continuing to clean our nets as we listened to this enigmatic figure speak about scripture and God's love.

Now I could blame it all on being tired and frustrated and being stuck in the boat with no means of escaping what was being said. In reality I couldn't escape without making a spectacle of myself in front of everyone who knew me by jumping overboard and wading back to shore. In truth I know the real reason I sat there with my head bowed to the nets trying not to catch the speaker's gaze, squirming as he sat on the edge of the boat addressing the crowd: his words were challenging; his words were commanding; his words demanded a response. I don't know whether everyone felt as convicted as I did, but I sensed all the terrible stuff in my life rising to the surface the longer I stayed in his presence, it was floating there like dung on the crystal clear water, but it felt like Jesus was offering to scoop it out and get rid of it. I don't know how else to describe it, but because all this stuff in my life was in my mind I felt so unworthy to be in this holy man's presence, and all I wanted to do was swim away.

Eventually he stopped speaking and turned to me and my brother. What he said next I'm guessing was so that he could get further away from the crowd who didn't seem to be getting the hint to disperse from the beach as they waited to follow him again once he climbed out of the boat, eager to hear more of what he had to say.

"Put out into deep water, and let down the nets for a catch."

'You're kidding', I thought to myself but didn't say. It was the last thing I wanted to do. More fishing! And with this… Jesus, who made me feel so full of sin that all I wanted to do was to run as far away from him as I could. But he asked, and how could I deny someone so majestic. "Master," I said, "we've worked hard all night and haven't caught anything. But because you say so, I will let down the nets."

Seeing that I was turning the boat out to go deeper John and James pushed their boat out to follow. I guess having listened to Jesus from the shore they were expectant of more and had the means to go where the crowd couldn't.

Andrew set to work arranging the nets while I rowed our boat a little further out. It didn't take long to get to deeper water as the lake was calm and still. To give you an idea of the size of the lake it might help you to know that it is also known as the Sea of Galilee. It is very wide and very deep, and on a good day is teeming with fish for many a fisherman like myself. I am well used to a big catch, but nothing prepared me for what happened next.

We let down our nets and before long a multitude of fish swam beneath the boat, it was as if they too were attracted to Jesus. There were so many that our nets began to break. That was when I was so glad that James and

John were close by. They came alongside us and helped pull up the nets, lowering their own for good measure. I had never seen a catch like it - none of us had. There were so many fish weighing down the boats we were really worried we might sink before we got back to shore.

With great haste we returned to the bank where Zebedee sat awaiting us. The crowds were gone by this time, presuming that we would be gone fishing for some while yet and they had lost their chance of hearing more from Jesus for the moment. With much effort we hauled and secured our catch. Wow, I thought I was tired before, now I was exhausted, but also exhilarated with the adrenalin pumping through me as I stood back from the boat with my feet on the sand staring at the wonder of my Lord.

Again that feeling of being unworthy rose up in a red heat from my toes to my cheeks and I trembled with embarrassment. I fell to my knees at Jesus' feet and said, "Go away from me, Lord; I am a sinful man!"

I couldn't be sure at the time, but having spoken to the others afterwards we all pretty much felt the same way.

Then Jesus said to me, "Don't be afraid; from now on you will fish for people."

I didn't quite get it at the time, 'you will fish for people'? I needed to learn more about this Jesus and his message to fully understand what he was calling us to do, but what we did understand was that he wanted us to follow him - there and then.

We pulled up our boats on the shore, and leaving them in the care of Zebedee, we left everything we had and followed Jesus. As crazy as it sounds, all four of us knew it was the right thing to do, and no matter what happened in the years that have passed since then, we've never looked back with regret. Following Jesus that day was the best thing I ever did.

JOHN'S DAY IN COURT
(MATTHEW 14:1-12   MARK 6:14-29)

The inner chambers of the royal palace were always a secretive place. Footsteps echoed in the lowly hallways away from the usual raucous clatter of the socialite hangers on, those seeking favours and status from the once imperial or influential house whom they'd aligned themselves within the now impoverished and powerless royal family. Then there were those who wished to get into the good graces of the oppressive force of occupiers who controlled the nation, willing in this means to sidle up to the titular tribal king, who had been allowed enough rope by means of wealth and majesty to believe he was still of importance and power. In truth, any strength and control he had was limited, and his law was only upheld at the command of the Roman garrison, to whose governor in Jerusalem King Herod willingly submitted his allegiance.

Herod Antipas, known as Herod the Tetrarch to most, was the son of Herod Magnus, the brutal king who had carried the title of Herod the Great. Herod the Great's kingdom had been divided upon his death, the occupying Roman Emperor, Caesar Augustus, allowing Herod's three sons to rule the divided kingdom under the control of the Empire: Philip ruled the territories east of the Jordan River, Archelaus ruled the area of Judea, and Antipas ruled the area of Galilee and Peraea.

Antipas was like so many other kings before him who had sunk to depraved practices and failed to lead the people in a godly manner, attributing to the demise of God's people. He followed evil practices: living an immoral life as he satisfied his own selfish hedonistic cravings of the flesh, and a lust for power and wealth he didn't deserve, all the while bowing down in obedience to whichever power or deity he thought might bestow on him the slightest token of thanks. He sought the wonder and awe of the mystics, the strength and command of the military strongholds, and the fear and respect of the people, which the law and tradition demanded. But in all this expectation the people despised him. The puppet king, who ruled none yet all in title alone, was a liar and a cheat. He decorated his domain with building projects to bolster his reputation yet cared little for the people themselves, unless they could serve his needs, and he made no attempt to hide his passions. And so the chambers hidden away from the banqueting hall were a lonely place, a dungeon for those in favour with the king in so much as the prison beneath the palace grounds was captivity for those who opposed him. The king and his family swam in their own filth of sin, trapped by their fame, and trapped by their own immoral lifestyle.

"The people are whispering about us." Her voice was muted so that her worried tones didn't echo off the cold stone walls of the empty passage between the royal bed chambers.

"My dear, the people are always whispering about us, it is their duty to grumble against their king."

"But we have too many enemies in our own court, my love; too many align themselves with your brother Philip."

"You are paranoid, my dear. You listen too much to the words of the prophet. Philip has his own kingdom and he would not dare challenge me for mine. There may be those in support of him, but at the fall of the sun they know who wears the crown on this side of the river. Let them speak what they will, I rule, not they."

"And what of me, my king? The people speak ill of me. They call me a whore and an adulterer. They will not say it to your face but I hear the whispers and the muttered grunts from those who are displeased with our actions."

"It will die down eventually my dear, Philip is no longer your husband, I am, and he will not rise up against me, and soon the people will accept us and forget our indiscretion."

"If only this were true, but I fear you are mistaken my king, for the people are being riled up by the prophet."

"Ignore him, he is a disgustingly diseased man. I honestly don't know why the people listen to such a fool. He spends his time by the water and stinks from his rough living. He washes others but fails to cleanse his own odour. They say he eats the insects and when he speaks the bugs fly from his mouth!"

"Yes, but the people still listen to him. He has a large following and he is swaying the opinion of the crowd."

King Herod paused in thought at the words of his wife, Herodias. "So, tell me, what is it the people say that has you so riled up?"

"As if you do not know, my lord, for I know even you like to hear him speak." The king gave his wife a sharp look with the flick of his head, forcing her to bow her head in submission. "They say John, the prophet, this baptiser of men, is condemning you, my lord, for taking me as your wife and is criticising our relationship."

He ruffled his brow and checked the darkened passage with a furtive scan, as though mistrusting his own abode. "How so?"

"John accuses the king of adultery, my lord. He says you should not have divorced your wife, Phasaelis, to be with me, and could not legally take me whilst my husband, your brother Philip, is still living. He says it goes against our laws."

"What would you have me do, kill my own brother? You know I will not."

"Of course, my love, but it may go a long way in silencing the rumour if the mouthpiece of the people were removed."

"Kill John?" He stepped back away from his wife in thought, then shook his head. "I would love nothing more than to have that disgusting cretin, that irritating trouble maker silenced permanently, but John is too popular, to kill him would cause more trouble for me. Even the Roman's would not come to my aid if I caused an uprising. They would see it as an internal matter not aimed at them so why should they interfere, and I could face the same fate as Archelaus and be deemed unfit to rule and have my kingdom stripped from me."

"Then have him arrested at least. You can hold him here in the palace cells where his poisonous tongue can be controlled, where he can no longer speak words against my king. Eventually the people will forget about him, and you will be stronger for it."

Herod gazed upon Herodias, her charm and wisdom pleased him. He need not provide John with a trial for his crimes for there were witnesses enough to testify that he was drumming up the crowd against the king, and inciting hatred towards his rule. His wife's plan was a good one. He smiled and turned away towards the banqueting hall, failing to see the look of spite that curled the lip of his queen as she allowed her hatred of the one who had spoken words against her to echo across her face.

John:

Is there no escape from this desert dust? Even here locked away within these four walls the grime of the land layers my clothes and matts the skin on my face. I miss the river to wash in, to bathe body and soul, to submerge and be cleansed, and to cleanse. Oh, how many need to hear the message of repentance and redemption? How many need to be pointed in the direction of the messiah? Have I done enough? My enemies surround me now, they have me captured and cornered where they can silence me; surely the number of my days are short.

They'll not starve me to death here at least, for even in a royal dungeon there are enough creatures to feed upon in the darkness. Not that I need to resort to stooping so low as even the scraps from the table of the king's servants are far greater than the mere morsels I allowed myself to indulge in as I wandered the path of the Jordan River. It wasn't that I wished to deprive myself of pleasures, it was just that speaking God's message to all who would listen was more important than my own desires. So look where that has got me, you may say, imprisoned with a grim future! But I am not disgruntled by the outcome, for I was obedient to what God had put on my heart and I knew, even from before I was born, that the presence of God was near me; to know him personally, to have embraced him, my Lord Jesus, is all the reward I need.

Some people call me a mad man, a wild preacher who roams the wilderness wearing rags and munching on locusts and yelling warnings of repentance as I baptise people in the river. It is those who refuse to hear the message who maintain that I have lost the plot and gone mad. Those that welcome God into their hearts and turn towards him receive his grace and mercy - it is they I tell to seek out Jesus - some do, some don't; each is on their own journey. You have to decide for yourself if what I say is crazy.

"Shut up you fool!"

That's Jaron Gannab. I think I'm the only one that calls him by his first name, everyone else just calls him Gannab, which means thief. He is in the next cell. He's a common street thief who has seen the inside of the cell more often than he's seen the mud walls of his own home. Despite his occupation he has some limited intelligence in the sense that he only steals from under the nose of Herod, and not the Romans. The Romans would dispense their justice much firmer with a cruel flogging or a crucifixion, but Herod finds his antics slightly amusing (so Jaron tells me) and so locks him away for periods of time. I have to say it doesn't surprise me, going on what I know of Herod. Herod doesn't always administer justice in its proper form and indulges like a greedy glutton in the desires of the flesh and the whims of his fancy. He likes to be amused and entertained and detests those who dare to criticise him. In that Jaron and Herod are the same, for Jaron doesn't like my ramblings either and often tries to silence me with insults.

Occasionally, if the wind is blowing in the right direction, I can hear the protests outside the palace grounds of those who follow me and demand my release. I am comforted by this for it keeps my spirits up knowing that I am not forgotten, and knowing that Herod, no matter how foolish he may be, is still fearful of the people rebelling against him, which would displease the Romans under whose authority he serves. So killing me now would not be in his best interest - certainly not while a rabble crowd is at his door. Yet more and more drift away to follow Jesus instead of me, which is good, for them at least.

I have lost track of how long I have been here now, months at least. I can no longer hear the voices of support from outside the gates and self-doubt has crept into my heart. Have I heard God clearly? Is Jesus who I think he is? He is my cousin, but is he also the messiah, or have I dreamt all that in my solitude and madness?

Jaron was released for a short while but he is back again now in his usual cell. He has filled my head with sinful thoughts, telling me that I have no followers left and that Jesus is hated by the religious leaders, and that Jesus is nothing but a political trouble maker using conjuring tricks to fool the crowd. I don't believe him, at least not all of it, but it would be the devil's work to intermix truth with lies so that it would be hard to distinguish the real truth.

I am lonely here. I am dirty here. I am cold here. I am fearful here. But God is here with me! Nothing can overcome me so long as I hold firm to that truth.

I had visitors a few days ago. Usually the guards won't allow people in to me out of fear of what I might say to them. They think I have a serpents tongue: quick to lick out to poison the establishment. The guards themselves have nothing against me personally, they're just following the orders that are issued from Herod. I talk to them often and have built a good rapport with them as we debate the scriptures and our expectations of the messiah and how he will affect the Roman occupation of our land. They are certainly more welcoming to what I have to say than Jaron.

"I heard that!"

"You were meant to!"

Herod himself is a bit of a conundrum. On the one hand he hates me and what I preach, and on the other he is intrigued and desperate to listen to what I have to say. He has come unannounced on various occasions and dismissed the guards so that he can stand in the shadows of the dank corridor listening to my ramblings as I shout at the walls - he probably thinks I don't know he's there, but I know, I can smell him; his perfumed stench wafts through into the cells.

Anyway, back to my visitors. It turns out I couldn't hear my supporters anymore because they had moved away from the side of the palace where the prison is housed and shifted their attention to the area of the palace where the royal chambers are situated. Herodias, troubled by the constant calls for my release had been growing quite anxious as much of the taunts were aimed at her and her illicit relationship with the king. Herod himself was quite happy to ignore the comments, the insults flowing off his back like water as he maintains an air of being above the law. He claims to be the Jewish king, but in truth he fails to practice our ways and has learned nothing of the failings of the fallen kings who preceded him. The only thing he fears is upsetting the Romans who can remove his power and replace him.

My visitors, close disciples who had stood with me in the river helping to organise the crowds, informed me that the rumour had spread that I was dead, that Herod had me killed in a rage at Herodias' bidding. It was no secret that the king's wife wanted rid of me and had taken my slur against her marriage to heart and sought to avenge my words. Word had reached Herod that the people were angry at the rumoured execution and were angrily camping outside the gates in protest. In order to prove the rumour false he had allowed my friends inside to see for themselves.

I was glad for their company, and to embrace my friends and to talk to other like-minded people who answered back where these cell walls remain silent to my voice.

"I wish you were silent!"

"If only you would listen to what I say, Jaron, and change your ways and repent then maybe you wouldn't keep ending up in here, held captive to your sin."

He'll be quiet now; he has no answer to the truth, but still his words about my Lord Jesus haunt me. So much so that I sent my friends away with a message. Despite what I have witnessed and what I know in my heart, I asked them to seek out Jesus and to ask him, to confirm with him, to reassure my doubting mind, that he is the one, the messiah that we have been waiting for. I don't expect an answer, for even as I spoke the words to my messengers I felt God's reassurance of the truth as I remembered the moment I baptised Jesus and the certainty of knowing who he was.

I guess part of me just wanted to know whether I had done enough, whether my mission was complete. All things now point towards him. I know deep down that I need to diminish in order for my followers to turn completely to him, so again I think it is a question I already know the answer to. I know ultimately what that means, I just don't know in what form it will take.

The weather has heated up over the last few weeks. The air is heavy and still, stagnant in the dank stench of these four walls. I can smell the sewage that runs along the gutter close to my feet.

Jaron has been given a job in the palace. He is still a prisoner and spends most of his nights in his cell, but for the rest of the time Herod has him chained to a post in the banquet hall, teasing him with food and fineries just within reach, playing a game where he can keep what he steals, but if Herod himself sees the theft it results in the severing of a digit. So far Jaron has lost two toes and a finger, much to the amusement of the king.

It is fair to say that Jaron has been less cocky in his attitude towards me of late, yet his stubborn aggressiveness hasn't evened his temper nor his willingness to admit his wrongdoings. It is through him that I have learned about the banquets that take place in the hall and how Herod lusts after Herodias' young daughter, Salome, with leering eyes. The thought of it makes me sick to my stomach; he is not satisfied with stealing one man's wife he now looks to her own daughter. There are lesser beasts out in the wilderness than in the court of the king.

I pray the king will turn from his ways, and I pray also that God will give me the strength to endure my captivity.

The Banquet Hall:

"But mother, the way he looks at me makes my skin crawl, it's disgusting."

"Don't be so precious, my darling. The king is a powerful man and what he wants he usually gets, eventually."

"Like you. You are both well suited mother."

"Tut tut my dear. I may tolerate your insolence to a degree but don't expect the king to be as patient with you, especially not on his birthday. Besides, you like to dance."

"I do, but not the way he wants me to. He doesn't appreciate the dance moves, he just wants to stare at my body."

"Yes, it is true the king has a rather grotesque appetite for such things I agree, but you must adhere to his wishes, if only for me."

The young teenager shook her head, the hair on her arms rising in protest as they stood on the edge of the great hall hidden in the shadows of an archway. Her mother, Herodias, grabbed her wrist and pulled her from where she stood and led her behind the nearest pillar out of sight of the baskets of food laid on the floor in front of where Herod reclined against a multitude of ornate and expensive cushions. Some servant girls lay with him and some of his closest advisers were laying nearby as they all watched a juggler tossing apples into the air. The king's eye had drifted from his wife and step-daughter long enough for his sodden mind to be drawn to the three fingered thief who sat chained to a far pillar. The thief sat motionless, having learned the lesson not to make a play for the food until the king had drunk enough to lack concentration; he was nearing that point but wasn't quite there yet.

"My daughter, I will do this thing for you: I will plough him with more drink so that both his eyes and his mind are blurry. He will applaud your dance but he will not appreciate it fully, nor admit that he is too drunk to see your beauty clearly. For this I ask one thing in return."

"Of course, mother, there is always something you want in return."

Herodias ignored the remark, they knew each other too well to dispute each other's character flaws, and anyway, she wanted her onside.

"When you go back in and he asks you again to dance for him, say yes, but on one condition - that he gives you whatever you ask for."

"He would never agree to it!"

"For you he will. Tease him. Hint at the idea so that he will think he has thought of it himself. He is in a good mood, celebrating and drinking, and pawing his hands over those girls. Trust me, if I know him as I think I do he will grant your wish, but make sure he declares it in front of everyone else loudly so that they all hear. Once he has agreed then dance for him, make it provocative and exciting so that he will be overly pleased and eager to fulfil your request. Afterwards, go to him and bid he keeps his promise, then return to me and I will tell you what to ask for."

The two female forms then slipped out from the shadows and reentered the hall with the expectation that all would play out as Herodias had predicted. Herodias filled the king's cup to overflowing and he drank greedily and in good spirits, and as his eyes fell upon her daughter, he begged the girl to dance before him.

Initially the girl refused, as she had done on numerous occasions before, but still the king persisted. Then with a teasingly seductive pout Salome teased her uncle with a promise to give him the dance of his life, so long as he granted her whatever she wished. The banquet hall erupted with laughter at her request, but his trusted advisers and friends who lay merry, and lacking in sober judgement, jeered in encouragement at the proposal until the king could see that it was the only way to have his birthday wish fulfilled. He nodded his consent but the girl lent forward with a cocked ear to show he needed to say the words. They were mumbled at first and still the girl jokingly maintained she could not hear. The cackles of the feast grew louder until, to be heard the king was forced through laughter of his own to shout his promise over the din of the court to honour the girl's desire if she danced for him.

And so she danced.

John:

I am comforted by the words Jesus sent back to me via my friends. He told me of the miracles being performed and the good news being proclaimed to the poor. To some this means nothing, but to me this is a glimpse of the kingdom of God here on Earth. I can rest assured that the messiah is here.

There is a lamp burning in the corridor just passed the jailers post. He's not there, neither is Jaron, the jailer took him up to the banquet hall earlier to help celebrate the king's birthday. I hope he is more successful than his last visit. His limp has got worse and the stump of toe looks infected. He has been feverous the last two days but I don't think the guards have noticed enough to care.

The empty corridor and cell next door is eerie as they echo the raucous behaviour from upstairs. I can hear muted instruments and laughter eclipsing the usual sounds of the night scratchings of creatures and insects scuttling about outside, and the wind howling through the trees, the calm of nature that I would usually drift off to sleep to. Tonight the winds of turmoil fill the palace, a heavy foreboding weights the air in my cell.

No one is here to hear my words, except my Lord God, who is with me always. He is my comfort, and will be until the end.

Salome:

His laugh is enough to make a dog sick. He drools and slobbers like a hungry hound with food tangled in the clumps of hair about his chin. How my mother can bare to go to his bed chambers I do not know. He leant so far forward trying to reach out to me as I danced he almost fell flat on his face. His subjects were trying to close the circle to force me closer to him but I'm not without my own talents in persuading men to move in the direction I wish them to go.

I kept the dance short as I could see his eyes glazed and unfocused. Without a doubt he enjoyed my performance, but he won't remember it for the most part I'm sure, but he will remember that I danced, especially when he finds out what he has promised to give me. Just to be sure that he was pleased with me, I asked him to repeat his pledge, which he did eagerly, readily and without thinking through the possible consequences, I'm sure if he had my mother's hand in it all may have been obvious. He even went as far as to offer me half the kingdom, though I doubt he would seriously expect me to request it, and I doubt he would uphold the request if I did - no, mother's proposal is more likely to be granted.

I guess I should be surprised and shocked by my mother's ruthless request, but I'm not; I should have known this was what she was after all along. There was a hint of pride in her eyes when she whispered to me what to ask my uncle for and she saw that I didn't flinch or even feign surprise. That's not to say that I am of the same mould as my mother, I still think what she has asked for is barbaric and cruel, but I'm just not surprised at the request.

Now I have the task of approaching the king whilst he reclines in good spirits and in the company of witnesses. I have little time, if I leave it too long he'll succumb to the grog and fall asleep amongst the revellers, and then he'll forget his promise.

I hope mother has judged this right and he won't react with anger and simply refuse the request. He doesn't like to lose face in his own court so he is unlikely to go against his own word made before all, not if it is something that can be granted immediately and without fuss, but still, I'm scared to ask for what mother wants.

King Herod:

Never has something sobered me so quickly. I feel as if I've been slapped in the face.

This is Herodias' doing. I can see her sneering face back in the shadows at the end of the hall. Oh, she has played me well. It is as if she herself had danced, not the younger more sprightful, and ageless version of my wife that I had leered over.

Feign deafness, or stupidity, or plain ignorance of what she's asking - just be dismissive.

Everybody's looking. I can feel the dumb flushed expression on my face at the shock of the request. Shake it off you oaf!

Everyone has heard her ask it. They've all gone quiet, looking to me, waiting for my reply.

I can't bear to look at her. Gone are those young innocent curves, the delicate skin and sweet smile, replaced is a devious weapon of betrayal.

How do I refuse? I cannot. I have promised. You drunken fool. This is going to cause me so much trouble. I swear if the people revolt Herodias will not hear the last of this!

Oh, I feel sick. I can feel it rising. No, it's just a belch.

Yes, you young harlot, I can see your pout of disgust beneath your flattering eyelashes that flutter with the tease your mother taught you.

"Sorry my dear, wha...what was it you asked for?"

"I want the head of the prisoner they call John the Baptist, and I want it now, brought in on a platter."

Yes, that's what I thought she said. Now everyone has heard it and there is no doubt about it - I am cornered.

She wants me to kill the one the people think is a prophet, the holy man. I will be fortunate if the people do not rise up against me for killing God's mouthpiece. I must sit back down. Oh, why did I stand up so readily to grant her request? Now it is all I can do to stop myself from falling.

Think your way out of it you fool. How can you deny her what she wants?

Stop nodding your head you idiot! Too late, you've agreed. Wave your hand and instruct the guard.

I need another drink. Someone get me another drink.

Jaron:

I no longer have a taste for being nimble fingered for the king's pleasure, not that I was much enjoying being his tortured toy to begin with. There is a painful sickness on me caused by my unattended wounds, but that is not what has turned my stomach this evening. I'm hoping the king will be too drunk to notice me sat here by the pillar. He is in too foul a mood now to treat me with any kindness and would most likely see me as joyful sport for the executioner's axe, especially as it has been employed once already this evening.

There was shock in the court when the platter was brought in, covered as a gift for Herodias' daughter. She seemed repulsed to be presented with such a trophy and quickly handed it over to her mother, who stood by her side. Overjoyed, she happily reached out and accepted the gift on behalf of her daughter.

There was a moment of stillness in the banquet hall as the cover was removed and John's head was held up and displayed for all to see. It was clear that she was making a statement not to question her position of intimacy next to the king, nor the actions of her and her husband. Well now we know who wears the trousers in this household and who controls the throne.

The silence lasted but a minute and then it became uncomfortable as the still warm blood that filled the plate spilled down her arms and onto the floor below. And then, as if to break the awkwardness, the king chuckled loudly, growing into a bellow that demanded accompaniment. Within seconds the guests were laughing with a forced banter which betrayed the hinted fear beneath as they all looked cautiously from the king to his wife and back again.

I know John's disciples will take it hard, not that I have much care for them or for the message he used to spout from his cell next to mine. In truth he was annoying, always trying to make me feel guilty and telling people that they were doing wrong and needed to stop. Pious do-good-er! But having said that, he didn't deserve what he got. He didn't even get a trial. They just dragged him out of his cell and put his head on a block.

I remember he kept going on about that bloke Jesus, how he was the messiah and we all needed to follow him. I wonder how him and his lot will take the news that John's been silenced for good? Maybe it will give them cause not to rock the boat with the establishment - if you upset those in charge they'll likely kill you for it, no matter how much truth is in your words, but then don't listen to me, what do I know, I'm just a thief they'll probably end up crucifying anyway.

TROAS
(ACTS 20:7-12)

Now you may have read some stories or heard of others tell of how they have seen the light at the end of the tunnel before coming back to life. Maybe some have told about how they lifted from their bodies and could look down upon themselves as they floated invisibly above in the air. Or maybe you have heard the tales of those who have described in great detail their trip to Heaven and the wonderful time they spent there with Jesus before being pulled back to earth. Well my story is nothing like that.

My account is not about some wild out of body experience but my true account of what happened to me one night long ago in a town called Troas.

I was only young then but the memory of what happened will never leave me.

There was this guy going around the area preaching the word about Jesus. He and his friends had been doing the rounds of the whole area and he had built up quite a reputation as a speaker and a great man devoted to God. He came to our town, Troas, but wasn't planning on staying long, in fact the night I heard him speak he was planning on leaving the very next day. Because of this the building we were in was packed to the rafters with people eager to hear what he had to say about Jesus and how we should live as followers of the true God.

We all met fairly early in the evening and broke bread together as Jesus had commanded us to do before his death, and then Paul began to speak.

As I said, it was quite packed in the place so everybody was squeezed in like sardines, and so I ended up being perched on the window ledge. Ok, some of you older folk might already be thinking that that's a pretty dumb place to sit: an open window (there was no glass remember, and the shutters were open to the cool night air), oh, and did I mention we were three floors up?

Paul certainly has a gift for talking. I mean, he went on and on and on. I was getting really uncomfortable sitting where I was and I could see others squirming in their seats as their legs went numb from sitting for so long. I could see loads of people yawning, not because what Paul was saying was boring, but because it was getting so late. You know how when you see someone yawning you can't help but do the same, well it was infectious: you could see it crossing the room like a Mexican wave. It didn't take long before I was breathing in deeply and sucking in a deep breath of a yawn, just like the one you're fighting off now I bet!

I kept with it for quite a while, but then my eyes began to get heavy. I fought the temptation to close them completely but eventually it felt so good to rest them and just let my ears tune into what was being said – it had been a long day after all.

Of course once you close your eyes it's quite hard to open them again, and then slowly your mind begins to shut down and your ears slowly tune out as your mind wanders and you drift off to sleep.

I think that if I had been sat on the floor with my friends then maybe they would have given me a prod to wake me up. You can always tell when someone has dropped off. Apart from the obvious eyes shut there is that deep breathing which often leads into a heavy snore that's always guaranteed to grab the humorous attention of your friends who will, most likely, snigger in a circle around you but eventually give you a gentle shake to avoid embarrassment and insult to the speaker.

But unfortunately I wasn't sat on the floor, and being in the window everyone else had their back to me so hadn't noticed me drift off.

There is another sensation you get when you drift off whilst in a seated position: that sensation of falling forward, when your head gets heavy and rolls towards your chest and you droop your body towards your knees. I felt this a couple of times as I sat there trying to listen to Paul, and each time I would snap my head up and rub my face and try to peel my eyes open to see if anyone had noticed me drop off. I think on one occasion I must have been overly conscious of my drooping head so much that I over compensated by leaning my head back. Of course in doing so my back arched trying to take the weight of my tipping head, over balancing me and pulling me out of my slumber. Had I been leaning against the wall this wouldn't have been a problem, but no, my back was to the open window. As my eyes snapped open to the falling sensation my legs flipped up in the air and I gave a scream of shock as I viewed the outside wall momentarily tumbling as I fell to the ground below.

I would like to say that I was ok, but I wasn't. In fact the fall killed me, pretty much instantly.

So how, I hear you ask, am I able to tell my story?

Paul, whilst talking later that night about some of Jesus' amazing miracles and how he saved people and continues to do so, pointed to me as an example of how we, in the name of our Lord Jesus, can do amazing things. "Just look at Eutychus," he said, and everyone in the room looked around at me in wonder as I sat there wide awake with a big beaming smile on my face – only this time I wasn't sat by the window!

So let's backtrack a bit. There I am lying dead on the ground and everyone comes out of the building calling my name and tearful. I'm a bloody mess. I don't know for sure but I guess my head got caved in on impact or my neck broke or something like that, I'm not totally sure, but there was enough blood on my clothes to suggest it was a nasty landing. No doubt about it – I was dead.

I don't remember being dead. I don't recall a bright light, or a voice guiding me, or a vision of Heaven. All I remember was waking up with Paul holding me in his arms praying.

It took a few moments for me to come to my senses but when I did Paul was smiling and I felt fine. I looked up to the window where I had been sat and then it dawned on me that I had fallen. I felt my body, knowing that I must have suffered a severe injury, but there wasn't a mark on me. Paul stood me to my feet, reassuring everyone that I was alive and not dead, and everyone marvelled at the miracle. At first none of us could believe it, but Paul simply turned and walked back inside the building and continued speaking to the crowd.

As I re-entered the room, one by one people were looking me up and down and then hugging me in disbelief. They could see the drying blood, could see I had no injuries, yet knew without a doubt that I had fallen from the window and that plenty of people testified to me being dead before Paul laid his hands on me.

Paul continued to talk throughout the night until the dawn broke, and the next day he left Troas. I never saw him again, but I haven't stopped telling my story ever since.

If you enjoyed reading this book then please leave a

review on Amazon or visit my webpage at:

www.cpclarke-author.com

This book is a collection of 13 biblical accounts told from the perspective of some of the lesser known characters in the Bible.

Ever wondered what Rahab thought about the Israelites when they came to Jericho, or what the soldiers thought of Paul when he was shipwrecked, or how about what was running through Sapphira's mind when she held back the money from the disciples? Get to read their point of view along with some other great bible characters.

Made in the USA
Charleston, SC
19 May 2016